Fresh Ways
with Fish & Shellfish

Time-Life Books Inc.
is a wholly owned subsidiary of
TIME INCORPORATED

FOUNDER: Henry R. Luce 1898-1967

Editor-in-Chief: Henry Anatole Grunwald
President: J. Richard Munro
Chairman of the Board: Ralph P. Davidson
Corporate Editor: Ray Cave
Group Vice President, Books: Reginald K. Brack Jr.
Vice President, Books: George Artandi

COVER
Baked sole takes on a whole new guise when it is wrapped around shrimp and asparagus and dressed with a purée of tomatoes, shallots and shrimp stock. Fresh dill provides additional flavor and color (recipe, page 36).

TIME-LIFE BOOKS INC.

EDITOR: George Constable
Director of Design: Louis Klein
Editorial General Manager: Neal Goff
Director of Editorial Resources: Phyllis K. Wise
Acting Text Director: Ellen Phillips
Editorial Board: Russell B. Adams Jr., Dale M. Brown, Roberta Conlan, Thomas H. Flaherty Jr., Donia Ann Steele, Rosalind Stubenberg, Kit van Tulleken, Henry Woodhead
Director of Photography and Research: John Conrad Weiser

PRESIDENT: Reginald K. Brack Jr.
Executive Vice Presidents: John M. Fahey Jr., Christopher T. Linen
Senior Vice President: James L. Mercer
Vice Presidents: Stephen L. Bair, Edward Brash, Ralph J. Cuomo, Juanita T. James, Hallett Johnson III, Robert H. Smith, Paul R. Stewart, Leopoldo Toralballa
Director of Production Services: Robert J. Passantino

Editorial Operations
Copy Chief: Diane Ullius
Editorial Operations: Caroline A. Boubin (manager)
Production: Celia Beattie
Quality Control: James J. Cox (director)
Library: Louise D. Forstall

Correspondents: Elisabeth Kraemer-Singh (Bonn); Dorothy Bacon (London); Maria Vincenza Aloisi, Josephine du Brusle (Paris); Ann Natanson (Rome).

Library of Congress Cataloguing in Publication Data
Main entry under title:
Fresh ways with fish & shellfish.
(Healthy home cooking)
Includes index.
1. Cookery (Fish) 2. Cookery (Shellfish) I. Time-Life Books.
II. Title: Fresh ways with fish and shellfish. III. Series.
TX747.F726 1986   641.6'92   86-4274
ISBN 0-8094-5816-0
ISBN 0-8094-5817-9 (lib. bdg.)

For information on and a full description of any Time-Life Books series, please write:
Reader Information
Time-Life Books
541 North Fairbanks Court
Chicago, Illinois 60611

Time-Life Books Inc. offers a wide range of fine recordings, including a *Big Bands* series. For subscription information, call 1-800-621-7026, or write TIME-LIFE MUSIC, Time & Life Building, Chicago, Illinois 60611.

HEALTHY HOME COOKING

SERIES DIRECTOR: Dale M. Brown
Deputy Editor: Barbara Fleming
Series Administrator: Elise Ritter Gibson
Designer: Herbert H. Quarmby
Picture Editor: Sally Collins
Photographer: Renée Comet
Text Editor: Allan Fallow
Editorial Assistant: Rebecca C. Christoffersen

Editorial Staff for *Fresh Ways with Fish and Shellfish:*
Book Manager: Susan Stuck
Assistant Picture Editor: Scarlet Cheng
Writer: Margery A. duMond
Researcher/Writer: Andrea E. Reynolds
Copy Coordinators: Marfé Ferguson, Elizabeth Graham, Norma Karlin
Picture Coordinator: Linda Yates
Photographer's Assistant: Rina M. Ganassa

Special Contributors: Mary Jane Blandford (food purchasing), Carol Gvozdich (nutrient analysis), Nancy Lendved (props), Tajvana Queen (kitchen assistant), Ann Ready (text), CiCi Williamson (microwave section)

THE COOKS

ADAM DE VITO began his cooking apprenticeship at L'Auberge Chez François near Washington, D.C., when he was only 14. He has worked at Washington's Le Pavillon restaurant, taught with cookbook author Madeleine Kamman, and conducted classes at L'Académie de Cuisine in Maryland.

HENRY GROSSI, who started his cooking career with a New York caterer, earned a Grand Diplôme at the École de Cuisine La Varenne in Paris. He then served as the school's assistant director and as its North American business and publications coordinator.

JOHN T. SHAFFER is a graduate of The Culinary Institute of America at Hyde Park, New York. He has had broad experience as a chef, including five years at The Four Seasons Hotel in Washington, D.C., where he was *chef saucier* at Aux Beaux Champs restaurant.

THE CONSULTANT

CAROL CUTLER lives in Washington, D.C., and is the prizewinning author of many cookbooks, including *The Six-Minute Soufflé and Other Culinary Delights* and *Pâté: The New Main Course for the 80's.* During the 12 years she lived in France, she studied at the Cordon Bleu and the École des Trois Gourmandes, as well as with private chefs. She is a member of the Cercle des Gourmettes as well as a charter member and past president of Les Dames d'Escoffier.

THE NUTRITION CONSULTANT

JANET TENNEY has been involved in nutrition and consumer affairs since she received her master's degree in human nutrition from Columbia University. She is the manager for developing and implementing nutritional programs for a major chain of supermarkets in the Washington, D.C., area.

SPECIAL CONSULTANT

JOYCE NETTLETON, who has a doctorate from the Harvard School of Public Health, is the author of *Seafood Nutrition,* a source book for the seafood industry and health and nutrition professionals. A registered dietician, she has produced several award-winning nutrition education booklets, promoted good nutrition on radio and television, and prepared a set of supermarket nutrition guidelines for the Food Marketing Institute and the Society for National Education. She lectures at Tufts University's Graduate School of Nutrition.

Nutritional analyses for *Fresh Ways with Fish and Shellfish* were derived from Practorcare's Nutriplanner System and other current data.

Other Publications:

UNDERSTANDING COMPUTERS
YOUR HOME
THE ENCHANTED WORLD
THE KODAK LIBRARY OF CREATIVE PHOTOGRAPHY
GREAT MEALS IN MINUTES
THE CIVIL WAR
PLANET EARTH
COLLECTOR'S LIBRARY OF THE CIVIL WAR
THE EPIC OF FLIGHT
THE GOOD COOK
WORLD WAR II
HOME REPAIR AND IMPROVEMENT
THE OLD WEST

This volume is one of a series of illustrated cookbooks that emphasize the preparation of healthful dishes for today's weight-conscious, nutrition-minded eaters.

Fresh Ways with Fish & Shellfish

BY

THE EDITORS OF TIME-LIFE BOOKS

TIME-LIFE BOOKS / ALEXANDRIA, VIRGINIA

Contents

Curried Grouper

Steamed, Spiced Crabs

Baked Whitefish with Garlic and Glazed Carrots

Clams and Rice Yucatan Style

4 Microwaving Fish and Shellfish.............113

Warm Scallop Salad with Cilantro Sauce

*Warm Mussel
and Potato Salad*

Lobster with Chanterelles and Madeira

A Most Excellent Food

The thought is as welcome as a breath of ocean air on a hot July day: Fish and shellfish contain more native goodness, ounce for ounce, than almost any other type of food. From the briny tang of a freshly shucked oyster to the majestic savor of a whole poached salmon, they are as healthful as they are delicious. Fish provide one of the most concentrated sources of high-quality protein, with an average four-ounce serving yielding up to half the daily dietary requirement of this nutrient. They deliver an uncommonly rich supply of vitamins and minerals as well, and they are easily digested.

At the same time, most varieties recommend themselves to weight-conscious diners. A four-ounce portion of haddock or cod, for example, has fewer than 100 calories. Even their fattier cousins, such as king salmon and shad, have fewer than half the calories of a T-bone steak. Moreover, nearly all fish and shellfish — and this comes as very good news indeed — are low in cholesterol. Even the folk wisdom that holds fish to be "brain food" may have some basis in fact: Recent studies have suggested that the fatty acids present in fish may be involved in the development of neural tissue.

More than 200 species of edible fish, not to mention a profusion of shellfish, thrive in North American waters. There is something to please every palate and accommodate every pocketbook. Flounder and sole have long been relished at the table, as have snapper and swordfish. But other, less well known fish are available, too, and they offer exciting culinary opportunities, as this book demonstrates. Much depends on the skill of the cook, to be sure, but it so happens that fish and shellfish are among the simplest of foods to prepare. Cooking times tend to be brief, and such basic methods as steaming, baking and broiling serve best to preserve nutrients and bring out flavors.

Some surprising discoveries

It has long been known that fish and shellfish bestow a generous nutritional dividend, but until quite recently no one knew just how significant the health payoff could be. The leaner varieties of fish have been prized for their modest amounts of calories and cholesterol, but the fattier types — with more than 5 percent of the edible portion of their bodies consisting of oil — have been cause for concern.

Now the picture has changed. Scientists turning their attention to the eating habits of Greenland Eskimos made a surprising discovery. During the first part of the 20th century, the Eskimos consumed, as they always had, great quantities of fatty fish and marine animals, yet they were astonishingly healthy. Despite their rich diet, heart disease was virtually unknown among them. A more recent study, in the Netherlands, corroborated this: A group of 852 middle-aged Dutch men, who had been eating modest but regular amounts of seafood over a 20-year period, had less than half the likelihood of contracting fatal heart disease than did their non-fish-eating compatriots — even though the fish eaters consumed slightly more cholesterol. Then, across the world in Japan, still another study showed that inhabitants of fishing villages, for whom fish was a staple, were virtually free of heart disease.

Fish and marine animals, the scientists determined, contain certain polyunsaturated fats found in no other foods, and these substances were demonstrated to have a profound effect on body chemistry. Fish oil appears to lower the levels of harmful triglycerides (or blood fats) in the blood. Moreover, it behaves quite differently from polyunsaturated vegetable oils in staving off heart disease. The oils from such rich-fleshed swimmers as salmon and mackerel actually discourage the formation of blood clots that can block ailing arteries. Nor is that all. Current studies suggest that fish oil may be beneficial in discouraging breast cancer and such inflammatory diseases as asthma and arthritis. The message comes through loud and clear: Fatty fish need not be avoided; their fat has virtues. And as if this were not enough to make seafood lovers smile, scientists have made some important discoveries about shellfish as well.

Improved analytical techniques have revealed not only that most shellfish are low in cholesterol but that some, notably the shelled mollusks, contain sterols picked up from their vegetarian diet that actually appear to reduce the amount of cholesterol absorbed by the body. Only squid, octopus, shrimp, razor clams, blue crab and black abalone have more than 100 milligrams of cholesterol per 3½-ounce portion; people on low-cholesterol diets should be wary of them, along with fish roe, which is also high in cholesterol.

Further enhancing the reputation of fish and shellfish for being healthful food are their stores of vitamins and minerals. The B vitamins, which the body needs to make proper use of protein and other nutrients, are particularly abundant in tuna, sardines, herring and various shellfish. Healthy blood requires iron and copper, and most shellfish provide both; finned fish with dark meat, such as mackerel, are also good iron sources. A generous dose of phosphorus, essential for strong bones, comes with every fish course. All salt-water varieties provide iodine, and most types provide potassium, fluoride, manganese and magnesium as well. Oysters are exceptionally high in zinc, which helps fight infection, promotes healthy skin, and is used to build more than 100 vital body enzymes.

Pursuing freshness

It goes without saying that fish tastes best when it has just been caught. The sweet dockside taste of a flounder or bass, plucked straight from the ocean and delivered on the plate with a minimum of preparatory fuss, is hard to equal. And for true fish lovers, nothing will do but that they go down to the water, fishing rod in hand, and haul in their own dinner. Even then they must take special care to maintain prime freshness. After shellfish, fish is the most perishable of foods. It has a high moisture content, offering bacteria an attractive environment in which to grow. In addition, oils present — particularly in the fattier types — begin to oxidize when they are exposed to air.

Knowledgeable anglers make it a practice to kill and gut each fish as soon as it is taken from the hook. A prompt execution — either by a smart blow on the head or else a quick slap against a hard object to break the backbone — is preferable to a lingering death in the fish well or on shore or bank. To gut the fish, make a cut from the anal fin toward the head and draw out the viscera *(techniques, pages 128 and 129);* bacteria lodged in the digestive organs are the first cause of decomposition. Stow the cleaned fish with ferns or seaweed in a creel or other container — or, better yet, in a cooler filled with crushed ice. Back in the kitchen, the fish can be scaled or skinned, or cut into fillets *(techniques, pages 128-131).* If not cooked immediately, it can be rinsed, patted dry, wrapped tightly in plastic and stored for three to five days in the coolest part of the refrigerator — but remember that it will lose a little of its freshness with each passing day.

Many people also like to gather their own shellfish, raking up clams from the shore, setting a crab line or lobster pot, or prying a feast of mussels from rocks or pilings. Provided that the source is an unpolluted body of water, untainted by human or industrial waste, the rewards at the table cannot be excelled. Be sure to check the local fish and game commission or the department of public health to be sure the area is safe. Whatever is collected can be preserved for a day or two in the refrigerator in open containers covered with a damp cloth, but do not keep it any longer.

What to look for

Most of us do our fishing at the market, but a few simple guidelines will help bring home the freshest catch available. The first priority is to find a reliable supplier — and the signs of the really good one are very evident. Every surface will be scrupulously clean, and a sweet, briny fragrance will fill the air. The fish will be laid out on ice in bins, or set in pans and kept just short of freezing. Most selections will have their heads kept on, and their skins will display a maritime rainbow of shimmering color. A good fishmonger will cut only as many fillets and steaks as he knows he can sell that day, for fish keeps best when left intact. There may be a tank of live lobsters in sea water, or a bin of iced crabs still twitching their claws. Turnover will be rapid, and what is on display today will usually be gone by tomorrow.

In making a choice for the dinner table, let your decision be guided by what is freshest. Clams and oysters should clamp up tightly when touched. Mussels, on the other hand, may keep their shells partly open, but these should stay rigidly in position. Lobsters and crabs should be lively. Squid should have firm, creamy-colored skin. When it comes to fish, good sense suggests a variety that is locally in season; it will tend to be both cheaper and fresher. But the nationwide distribution of commercial fish has become so efficient, with daily shipments sent out from processing centers by refrigerated truck or airplane, that a wide selection is usually available. Aquaculture has increased the year-round availability of certain species such as rainbow trout, catfish and salmon. These farm-grown specimens are scientifically fed, then harvested when they reach a certain size and sent immediately to market.

Fresh fish is sold drawn — that is, scaled, with the viscera and gills removed — or dressed: drawn, with the head, tail and fins removed. More often, the fish will be steaked — cut into cross-sections — or filleted. Buying a whole drawn fish has advantages; it will have been handled less and will have lost fewer of its juices. Photographs on pages 130 and 131 show how you can slice your own fillets from whole fish.

When a whole fish is truly fresh, its eyes are clear, bright and slightly protruding, with shiny black pupils. The gills are pinkish or bright red; brown gills signal a shopworn specimen. The skin will

The Key to Better Eating

Healthy Home Cooking addresses the concerns of today's weight-conscious, health-minded cooks with recipes that take into account guidelines set by nutritionists. The secret to eating well, of course, has to do with maintaining a balance of foods in the diet. The recipes thus should be used thoughtfully, in the context of a day's eating. To make the choice easier, this book presents an analysis of nutrients in a single serving of each fish or shellfish recipe, as at right. The counts for calories, protein, cholesterol, total fat, saturated fat and sodium are approximate. Among other things, the fat content of fish can vary, depending on the season, where the fish was caught, and the species. For fish cooked with the skin on, data are not yet available for the skin's calories and fat.

Interpreting the chart

The chart below shows the National Research Council's Recommended Dietary Allowances of calories and protein for healthy men, women and children, along with the council's recommendations for the "safe and adequate" maximum intake of sodium. Although the council has not established recommendations for either cholesterol or fat, the chart does include what the National Institutes of Health and the American Heart Association consider the daily maximum amounts of these for healthy members of the general population.

The volumes in the Healthy Home Cooking series do not purport to be diet books, nor do they focus on health foods. Rather, they express a commonsense approach to cooking that uses salt, sugar, cream, butter and oil in moderation while employing other ingredients that also provide flavor and satisfaction. Herbs, spices and aromatic vegetables, as well as fruits, peels, juices, wines and vinegars are all employed toward this end.

The recipes make few unusual demands. Naturally they call for fresh ingredients, offering substitutes when these are unavailable. (Only the original ingredient is calculat-

---

Calories **180**
Protein **21g.**
Cholesterol **65mg.**
Total fat **8g.**
Saturated fat **4g.**
Sodium **230mg.**

---

ed in the nutrient analysis, however.) Most of the ingredients can be found in any well-stocked supermarket.

In order to simplify meal planning, most of the recipes offer accompaniments. These accompaniments are intended only as suggestions, however; cooks should let their imaginations be their guide and come up with ideas of their own to achieve a sensible and appealing balance of foods.

In Healthy Home Cooking's test kitchens, heavy-bottomed pots and pans are used to guard against burning the food whenever a small amount of oil is used and where there is danger of the food adhering to the hot surface, but nonstick pans can be utilized as well. Both safflower oil and virgin olive oil are favored for sautéing. Safflower oil was chosen because it is the most highly polyunsaturated vegetable fat available in supermar-

kets, and polyunsaturated fats reduce blood cholesterol. Virgin olive oil is used because it has a fine fruity flavor lacking in the lesser grade known as "pure." In addition, it is — like all olive oil — high in monounsaturated fats, which do not increase blood cholesterol and, according to recent research, may even lower it. When virgin olive oil is unavailable, or when its flavor is not essential to the success of the dish, "pure" may be used.

About cooking times

To help the cook plan ahead, Healthy Home Cooking takes time into account in its recipes. While recognizing that everyone cooks at a different speed, and that stoves and ovens differ, the series provides approximate "working" and "total" times for every dish. Working time stands for the minutes actively spent on preparation; total time includes unattended cooking time, as well as time devoted to marinating, steeping or soaking ingredients. Since the recipes emphasize fresh foods, they may take a bit longer to prepare than "quick and easy" dishes that call for canned or packaged products, but the payoff in flavor, and often in nutrition, should compensate for the little extra time involved.

Recommended Dietary Guidelines

		Average Daily Intake		Maximum Daily Intake			
		CALORIES	PROTEIN grams	CHOLESTEROL milligrams	TOTAL FAT grams	SATURATED FAT grams	SODIUM milligrams
Children	7-10	2400	22	240	80	27	1800
Females	11-14	2200	37	220	73	24	2700
	15-18	2100	44	210	70	23	2700
	19-22	2100	44	300	70	23	3300
	23-50	2000	44	300	67	22	3300
	51-75	1800	44	300	60	20	3300
Males	11-14	2700	36	270	90	30	2700
	15-18	2800	56	280	93	31	2700
	19-22	2900	56	300	97	32	3300
	23-50	2700	56	300	90	30	3300
	51-75	2400	56	300	80	27	3300

be firm and bright. The scales will adhere to it tightly. The flesh of most fish will feel firm and elastic to the touch. And a fresh fish smells fresh, with a subtle clean fragrance suggestive to some of cucumber, to others of the sea itself. A fishy odor is a sure sign of deterioration. Members of the shark and skate families give off a slight ammonia scent, but this is natural and will disappear.

The task of identifying truly fresh fish is more difficult when it comes to steaks or fillets. But here, too, appearances count. Each piece should be firm and its cut surfaces should be moist, not dried out, with no sliminess and no browning or yellowing at the edges. Nor should there be any smell of fishiness. If the fish is prepackaged, there should be little air space between the fish and wrapping, and little or no liquid in the package (pass up any fish in milky-colored fluid).

When fresh fish fail to meet these criteria, a frozen specimen may be the preferred option. Indeed, most fish caught in the United States is sold this way. But bear in mind that any intermediate thawing and refreezing between the processing center and the store counter (or between the home freezer and table, for that matter) take an unfortunate toll. Buy only frozen packages that are solid, without interior air pockets. Reject any that have torn wrappings or exterior coatings of frost. Discoloration of the fish is a telltale sign of freezer burn, which occurs when moisture is lost through faulty packaging and which destroys flavor.

The amount of seafood to buy, whether frozen or fresh, depends on how it will be cooked, and of course on how much is to be eaten. A standard portion of fish or shellfish runs about four to six ounces of cooked meat, not counting bones or shells (this book emphasizes a four-ounce serving). Thus, if a fish is to be purchased whole, you should allow as much as three quarters of a pound for each diner; if already dressed, about half a pound per person will be ample. Half a dozen clams or oysters make the customary half-shell first course. When buying fresh shrimp, remember that about half their weight consists of heads and shells.

Ensuring flavor and nutrition

Once home from the market, seafood tastes best when it is promptly used. If fish cannot be cooked on the day of its purchase, it should be rinsed in cold water, dried with paper towels, swathed tightly in plastic wrap and stored for up to two days in the coolest part of the refrigerator.

Longer intervals of storage require that the fish be frozen. Whether it is purchased at the store or proudly borne home from a morning's fishing expedition, the method is the same. The gutted fish should be scaled, if necessary; it can then be cut into fillets, steaks or chunks, or kept whole, as desired. After rinsing the fish under cold running water, pat it dry with paper towels and wrap it in aluminum foil or moistureproof plastic, with as much air excluded as possible; air is the archvillain of freezer burn. The packets should be spaced loosely in the freezer to promote rapid chilling. If freezer temperatures are held down to a frigid 0° F., fatty fish can be stored for up to three months, and leaner varieties for six months. But for the best flavor, all frozen fish should be served within one or two months. Do not attempt to freeze shellfish; some, like shrimp, may have already been frozen because of their perishability. Refreezing them will serve only to rob them of more flavor and texture.

In thawing fish, proceed slowly. Defrost each packet in the refrigerator, well in advance of the time the fish is to be cooked; allow 24 hours for each pound. Do not thaw fish at room temperature; bacteria will quickly start to grow. Once the fish is defrosted, wash it again gently and dry it once more to get rid of any bacteria that might be present on the surface.

No matter how carefully a potential seafood dinner has been selected or stored, its moment of truth comes in the kitchen. The role of the cook is much like that of a classical pianist: to render fully each nuance of texture and flavor, with verve and freshness, but without undue violence or distortion. The recipes in this book are designed to do just that. They rely on basic, easily mastered cooking methods that work most effectively in transmitting both nutrients and taste. Only deep frying is omitted, for obvious health reasons. (Nor is the eating of raw fresh-water fish recommended, because of the possibility of parasites.) The first section takes up the lean varieties of finfish, along with the cooking methods that suit them best. Their fattier relatives are discussed in the second section. Shellfish are the focus of the third section, and the final section introduces the special procedures for cooking fish and shellfish in a microwave oven. A glossary, beginning on page 137, defines and describes all the fish and shellfish called for by the recipes in the book.

Since they are naturally tender, fish and shellfish benefit from short cooking times. The recipes give specific heats, and most recommend that you test the fish for doneness after the indicated time. A reliable guideline for cooking fish is the rule developed by Canada's Department of Fisheries: For all cooking methods, give the fish 10 minutes for every inch of flesh measured at its thickest point. (When baking, set the oven at 450° F.) Not only is it essential that fish and shellfish be cooked carefully, but also that they be served right away.

In the recipes that follow, sauces are kept light and delicate — designed to enhance, not mask, the seafood's innate goodness. They often incorporate the fish's juices or depend on fish stock for subtlety of flavor (a recipe for fish stock appears on page 136). An inventive scheme of seasonings and sauce bases replaces the calorie-charged elaborations of tradition. Delivered to the table with its virtues intact, each dish seems to carry with it the roar of the surf or the gurgle of the trout stream.

1 *Fresh from the sea, lean fish — bass, red drum, flounder, red snapper and tilefish among others — shimmer on a bed of shaved ice.*

Beneficent, Lean-Fleshed Fish

More low-fat fish come to market year round than any other kind — and no wonder. They are among the most popular of commonly eaten salt-water and fresh-water specimens. All are rich in protein and miserly in calories, with a fat content of no more than five percent and frequently of less than two percent. The fat they do possess is found mainly in the liver, which is removed in cleaning.

Lean fish tend to be mild in flavor, with tender, flaky white or pale flesh that lends itself to varied culinary treatments. But because lean fish tend to dry out during cooking, techniques that preserve or add moisture — notably sautéing or steaming — are ideal. Most varieties may also be cooked successfully in the oven, provided they are supplied with additional moisture, smothered in a blanket of vegetables, or wrapped in parchment paper or foil so that they can steam in their own juices. Some may even be broiled or grilled, if they are generously basted.

Among the leanest of the lean are such flatfish as flounder and sole, with their pancake-like bodies and delicate, fine-textured flesh. One of the nicest things about flatfish is that they may be substituted for one another in a dish. What is more, they are relatively easy to prepare; photographs on page 131 show how to fillet and skin them.

Techniques for dressing and filleting lean round-fish — so described because their bodies are tubular in shape — are demonstrated on pages 128-130. In this section, such ever-popular roundfish as cod and haddock get fresh treatment. Codfish made into cakes acquire new character when served with a horseradish sauce, and haddock is transformed when baked in enchiladas topped with chopped tomatillos and chilies.

Enterprising cooks who would like to try less familiar fish will find interesting recipes for several varieties. One of these calls for mahimahi, a brightly scaled denizen of subtropical waters; the fish is stuffed with a spicy filling, baked and then topped with sliced, toasted almonds. Skate is poached, and the poaching liquid becomes the base for a vinaigrette-like sauce containing slices of crunchy green beans and sweet red pepper. Shark, long shunned at American tables but now receiving deserved attention from adventurous cooks, is stir fried with Nappa cabbage in a mild dish that belies this predator's nasty reputation. One bite into a piece of shark so prepared will prove that eating it amounts to sweet revenge indeed.

White Sea Bass with 20 Cloves of Garlic

Serves 4
Working time: about 20 minutes
Total time: about 1 hour

Calories **200**
Protein **23g.**
Cholesterol **47mg.**
Total fat **10g.**
Saturated fat **1g.**
Sodium **210mg.**

1¼ lb. Pacific white sea bass steaks (or halibut)
2 tbsp. safflower oil
2 red peppers, diced
20 garlic cloves, very thinly sliced
1 jalapeño pepper, seeded and finely chopped (caution, page 41)
6 tbsp. finely chopped cilantro, plus several whole sprigs for garnish
¼ tsp. salt
freshly ground black pepper
1 tsp. paprika, preferably Hungarian
2 cups fish stock (recipe, page 136) or dry white wine

Rinse the fish under cold running water and pat it dry with paper towels. Remove any scales from the skin; if the steaks are large, cut them in half lengthwise.

Heat the oil over medium heat in a heavy-bottomed skillet large enough to hold the fish in one layer. Add the red pepper and sauté it lightly for two minutes. Add the garlic, jalapeño pepper and chopped cilantro; reduce the heat to low and cook, stirring frequently, for one minute. Place the fish on top of the vegetables and sprinkle it with the salt, some pepper and the paprika. Pour in the stock or wine and bring the liquid to a simmer, basting the fish occasionally. Cover the skillet and reduce the heat to low. Cook the fish until it is opaque — about eight minutes.

With a slotted spoon, transfer the fish to a deep platter. Remove the skin from the steaks. Cover the platter with aluminum foil to keep the fish from drying out while you finish the sauce.

Boil the liquid in the skillet, stirring occasionally, until only about ½ cup remains — five to 10 minutes. Pour the sauce over the fish. Serve the fish at room temperature or cold, garnished with the cilantro sprigs.

SUGGESTED ACCOMPANIMENTS: *green salad; sourdough rolls.*

Pike with Onions, Cabbage and Apple

Serves 6
Working time: about 25 minutes
Total time: about 1 hour

Calories **200**
Protein **18g.**
Cholesterol **52mg.**
Total fat **6g.**
Saturated fat **2g.**
Sodium **145mg.**

one 3-lb. pike (or walleye)
1 tbsp. safflower oil
3 onions, thinly sliced
2 cups thinly sliced cabbage (about ½ lb.)
1 cup dry white wine
1 tbsp. cider vinegar
¼ tsp. caraway seeds
¼ tsp. salt
freshly ground black pepper
1 red apple, cored and cut into thin wedges
1½ tbsp. unsalted butter
1 tbsp. finely cut chives

To loosen the scales of the pike, scald the fish: Put it in the sink or a large basin and pour a kettle of boiling water over it. Scale and clean the fish *(technique, pages 128-129)*. Cut off and discard the head.

Preheat the oven to 450° F. Heat the oil in a large, heavy-bottomed skillet over medium-high heat. Add the onions and sauté them until they are translucent — about four minutes. Add the cabbage, wine, vinegar, caraway seeds, salt and some pepper, and stir well. Bring the liquid to a boil, then reduce the heat to medium and simmer the mixture for 10 minutes.

Transfer the vegetable mixture to a baking dish large enough to accommodate the pike. Set the pike on top of the vegetables and arrange the apple wedges around it. Bake the fish until the flesh is opaque and feels firm to the touch — about 20 minutes.

Transfer the pike and the apples to a heated serving platter and cover them with aluminum foil; set the platter aside while you finish cooking the cabbage and onions. Return the cabbage-and-onion mixture to the skillet and cook it over high heat until only about ¼ cup of liquid remains — approximately 10 minutes. Add the butter and stir until it melts. Place the vegetables around the fish on the serving platter, sprinkle the chives over the fish and serve immediately.

SUGGESTED ACCOMPANIMENTS: *wild-rice pilaf; lima beans.*

Repeat these steps with the remaining fillets. Drizzle any remaining garlic butter over the top.

Bake the fish until it feels firm to the touch and the coating is golden brown — 10 to 12 minutes. Serve immediately.

SUGGESTED ACCOMPANIMENTS: *tomato salad; green beans.*

Crisp Baked Porgies with Tomato and Mint

Serves 4
Working time: about 25 minutes
Total time: about 40 minutes

Calories **280**
Protein **22g.**
Cholesterol **58mg.**
Total fat **15g.**
Saturated fat **3g.**
Sodium **210mg.**

4 porgies (or croaker or perch), about ½ lb. each, dressed (techniques, pages 128-129)
½ cup skim milk
1 egg white, beaten
⅓ cup cornmeal
¼ cup sliced blanched almonds, chopped
½ cup chopped fresh mint
1 scallion, trimmed and thinly sliced
freshly ground black pepper
1 tbsp. safflower oil
1 tbsp. unsalted butter
¼ tsp. salt
2 large ripe tomatoes, peeled, seeded and finely chopped
1 tbsp. fresh lime or lemon juice
1 tbsp. red wine vinegar

Rinse the dressed porgies under cold running water and pat them dry. Mix the milk and egg white in a shallow bowl. Soak the fish in this mixture for 15 minutes, turning them twice. Preheat the oven to 350° F.

While the porgies are soaking, combine the cornmeal, almonds, ¼ cup of the mint, the scallion and a generous grinding of pepper in a shallow dish. At the end of the soaking time, dredge each porgy in the cornmeal mixture to coat it evenly.

Heat the oil and butter in a large ovenproof skillet (preferably one with a nonstick surface) over medium heat. Add the porgies and cook them on the first side for four minutes. Sprinkle the fish with ⅛ teaspoon of the salt and turn them over; sprinkle them with the remaining ⅛ teaspoon of salt and cook them on the second side for two minutes. Put the skillet in the oven for 15 minutes to finish cooking the porgies.

While the fish are baking, make the sauce: Combine the tomatoes, the remaining ¼ cup of mint, the lime or lemon juice, the vinegar and some pepper in a bowl.

When the porgies are done, transfer them to a serving platter; pass the sauce separately.

SUGGESTED ACCOMPANIMENTS: *corn on the cob.*

Black Sea Bass Fillets with Cracked Anise and Mustard Seeds

Serves 4
Working time: about 15 minutes
Total time: about 25 minutes

Calories **190**
Protein **22g.**
Cholesterol **62mg.**
Total fat **9g.**
Saturated fat **4g.**
Sodium **230mg.**

two skinned black sea bass fillets (or rockfish), about ½ lb. each, cut in half on the diagonal
1 shallot, finely chopped
2 tsp. anise or fennel seeds
1 tbsp. mustard seeds
⅓ cup dry bread crumbs
2 tsp. fresh thyme, or ½ tsp. dried thyme leaves
freshly ground black pepper
2 tbsp. unsalted butter
1 garlic clove, very finely chopped
juice of ½ lemon
¼ tsp. salt

Preheat the oven to 500° F. Lightly butter the bottom of a heavy, shallow baking dish. Sprinkle the chopped shallot into the dish.

Crack the anise or fennel seeds and the mustard seeds with a mortar and pestle, or on a cutting board with the flat of a heavy knife. Transfer the seeds to a wide, shallow bowl or pan, and combine them with the bread crumbs, thyme and some pepper. Put the butter and garlic into a saucepan and melt the butter.

Rinse the fillets under cold running water and pat them dry with paper towels. Rub the fillets with the lemon juice and sprinkle them with the salt and some pepper. Brush a fillet on both sides with some of the garlic butter, then coat it well with the bread-crumb mixture and lay it on the shallot in the baking dish.

Striped Bass on a Bed of Mushrooms and Spinach

Serves 4
Working (and total) time: about 35 minutes

Calories **185**
Protein **24g.**
Cholesterol **91mg.**
Total fat **6g.**
Saturated fat **1g.**
Sodium **260mg.**

1 lb. striped bass fillets (or black sea bass, red snapper or rockfish), skin left on
12 oz. mushrooms, wiped clean and sliced
juice of 1 lemon
freshly ground black pepper
1 lb. fresh spinach, washed and stemmed, or 10 oz. frozen spinach, thawed
1 tbsp. safflower oil
1 onion, finely chopped
⅛ tsp. grated nutmeg
¼ tsp. salt

Put the mushrooms in a saucepan with the lemon juice and a generous grinding of pepper. Pour in enough water to cover them, then bring the liquid to a boil. Reduce the heat to medium and simmer the mixture until the mushrooms are tender — about five minutes. Set the pan aside.

Put the fresh spinach, with water still clinging to its leaves, in a large pot over medium heat. Cover the pot and steam the spinach until the leaves are wilted — two to three minutes. (Frozen spinach needs no cooking.) Squeeze the moisture from the spinach and chop it coarsely.

Heat the oil in a large, heavy-bottomed skillet over medium heat. Add the onion and cook it until it is translucent — about four minutes. Drain the mushrooms and add them to the skillet, then stir in the spinach and cook for two minutes. Season the mixture with the nutmeg, salt and some additional pepper, then spread it evenly in the bottom of a flameproof baking dish.

Preheat the broiler. Rinse the fillets under cold running water and pat them dry with paper towels. Lay the fillets skin side up on the vegetable mixture. Broil the fish until the flesh feels firm to the touch and the skin is crisp — about five minutes. Serve immediately.

SUGGESTED ACCOMPANIMENT: *sautéed sliced turnips.*

Indian-Spiced Monkfish

Serves 4
Working time: about 25 minutes
Total time: about 40 minutes

Calories **240**	1 lb. monkfish fillets
Protein **22g.**	juice of 2 lemons
Cholesterol **43mg.**	4 garlic cloves, chopped
Total fat **10g.**	1 tbsp. chopped fresh ginger
Saturated fat **1g.**	2 tbsp. chopped cilantro
Sodium **420mg.**	1 tsp. coriander seeds
	1 tsp. ground turmeric
	1 tsp. dark brown sugar
	½ tsp. cumin seeds
	¼ tsp. mustard seeds
	¼ tsp. salt
	2 tbsp. safflower oil
	1 onion, finely chopped
	¾ cup plain low-fat yogurt
	¾ cup dry bread crumbs

In a blender, purée the lemon juice, garlic, ginger, cilantro, coriander seeds, turmeric, brown sugar, cumin seeds, mustard seeds and salt. (Alternatively, grind the seasonings by hand in a mortar and pestle, then stir in the lemon juice.)

Heat 1 tablespoon of the oil in a heavy-bottomed skillet. Add the onion and cook it until it is translucent — about four minutes. Add the spice purée and cook for three minutes more. Remove the skillet from the heat and set it aside.

Preheat the broiler. Rinse the fish and pat it dry with paper towels. Slice the fillets crosswise into pieces about 2 inches wide.

Transfer the contents of the skillet to a bowl and mix in the yogurt. Transfer half of this yogurt mixture to a small serving bowl and set it aside. Use the other half of the mixture to coat the fish: Dip a piece of fish first in the yogurt, then in the bread crumbs, covering it completely. Put the piece in a flameproof baking dish. Repeat the process with the remaining pieces.

Drizzle the remaining tablespoon of oil over the fish. Broil the fish 3 inches below the heat source for about three minutes on each side. Set the oven temperature at 450° F. Transfer the dish to the oven and bake the fish until it feels firm to the touch — approximately 10 minutes. With a spatula, carefully remove the pieces from the baking dish. Serve the monkfish with the reserved yogurt sauce.

SUGGESTED ACCOMPANIMENT: *cucumber salad.*

Monkfish with Artichoke Ragout

THIS DISH WAS INSPIRED BY "RAÏTO," A PROVENÇAL SAUCE
OF TOMATOES, RED WINE, CAPERS AND BLACK OLIVES.

Serves 4
Working time: about 40 minutes
Total time: about 1 hour

Calories **260**
Protein **21g.**
Cholesterol **40mg.**
Total fat **8g.**
Saturated fat **1g.**
Sodium **430mg.**

1 lb. monkfish fillets
¼ cup distilled white vinegar
4 artichokes
1½ tbsp. virgin olive oil
1 onion, finely chopped
4 garlic cloves, chopped
1 cup red wine
2½ lb. ripe tomatoes, peeled, seeded and coarsely chopped, or 28 oz. canned tomatoes, chopped, the juice reserved
6 oil-cured black olives, pitted and halved
½ tsp. capers
1 bay leaf

Pour enough water into a nonreactive saucepan to fill it about 2 inches deep. Add the vinegar to the water.

To prepare the artichoke bottoms, first break or cut the stem off one of the artichokes. Snap off and discard the outer leaves, starting at the base and continuing until you reach the pale yellow leaves at the core. Cut the top two thirds off the artichoke. Using a paring knife, shave off any dark green leaf bases that remain on the artichoke bottom. Cut the bottom into quarters; trim away any purple leaves and the fuzzy choke. Then cut each quarter into four wedges and drop them into the vinegar water in the saucepan. Repeat these steps with the remaining artichokes.

Simmer the artichoke bottoms over medium heat until they are tender — about 15 minutes. Drain them and set them aside.

Rinse the fillets and pat them dry; slice them into pieces 1½ inches wide. Pour the oil into a large, heavy-bottomed skillet over high heat. Add the monkfish pieces and sear them for one minute on each side. Transfer the fish to a plate and set it aside.

Reduce the heat to medium high and cook the onion in the skillet until it is translucent — about four minutes. Stir in the garlic and cook for one minute longer. Pour in the wine and cook it until almost no liquid remains — about five minutes. Stir in the tomatoes (and the reserved juice if you are using canned tomatoes), the olives, capers and bay leaf. Bring the liquid to a boil and cook it until it is reduced by half — about five minutes more.

Put the artichoke pieces in the sauce and set the monkfish pieces on top. Reduce the heat to medium, cover the pan, and cook the fish until it is opaque and feels firm to the touch — about 10 minutes. Transfer the fish to a serving dish. Raise the heat to high and cook the sauce for one or two minutes to thicken it. Transfer the artichokes to the serving dish; pour the sauce over the artichokes and fish, and serve at once.

Salad of Tilefish and Wild Rice

Serves 8
Working time: about 25 minutes
Total time: about 2 hours

Calories **310**
Protein **18g.**
Cholesterol **28mg.**
Total fat **8g.**
Saturated fat **1g.**
Sodium **300mg.**

1 lb. skinned tilefish fillet (or grouper, orange roughy or red drum)
1 cup fish stock or court bouillon (recipes, page 136)
¼ cup chopped shallots
2 garlic cloves, finely chopped
1½ tbsp. chopped fresh sage, or 1½ tsp. ground sage
½ tsp. salt
freshly ground black pepper
1½ cups wild rice
1 cup dry white wine
juice of 1 lemon
1 cup baby lima beans, thawed if frozen
¼ cup thinly sliced sun-dried tomatoes
½ lb. snow peas, strings removed, pods cut diagonally in half
3 tbsp. virgin olive oil

Pour the stock or court bouillon and 1¾ cups of water into a large saucepan. Add 2 tablespoons of the shallots, half of the garlic and half of the sage, ¼ teaspoon of the salt and some pepper; bring the liquid to a boil. Stir in the rice, reduce the heat to low and partially cover the pan. Simmer the rice with the lid slightly ajar until the rice has absorbed the liquid and is tender — 40 to 50 minutes.

While the rice is cooking, prepare the poaching liquid. In a large, nonreactive skillet over medium heat, ▶

combine the wine, ½ cup of water, the lemon juice, the remaining 2 tablespoons of shallots, the remaining garlic and sage, and the remaining ¼ teaspoon of salt. Grind in a generous amount of pepper.

While the poaching liquid heats, rinse the fillet under cold running water; if the fillet is too large to fit into the skillet in one piece, cut it in half. When the poaching liquid is hot, reduce the heat to low and place the fish in the liquid. Gently poach the fish for six minutes on the first side, then turn it over and cook it until the flesh just flakes — three to four minutes more.

Transfer the fish to a plate. Let it cool slightly, then refrigerate it. Do not discard the poaching liquid.

When the rice is done, refrigerate it in a large mixing bowl. Increase the heat to high and boil the poaching liquid for one minute to reduce it slightly. Add the lima beans and tomatoes, and cook them for three minutes. Stir in the snow peas and cook the mixture for one minute more, stirring constantly; there should be just 2 or 3 tablespoons of liquid remaining.

With a slotted spoon, transfer the vegetables to the bowl with the rice. Whisk the oil into the reduced liquid in the skillet and pour this sauce over the rice and vegetables. Toss together well. Flake the fish into the bowl and gently toss the salad once more. Serve at room temperature or chilled.

SUGGESTED ACCOMPANIMENT: *fruit salad.*

Sea Trout Baked in Phyllo

Serves 6
Working time: about 45 minutes
Total time: about 1 hour 20 minutes

Calories **450**
Protein **32g.**
Cholesterol **132mg.**
Total fat **18g.**
Saturated fat **4g.**
Sodium **290mg.**

one 4-lb. sea trout (or salmon or striped bass), scaled and filleted (technique, page 130), the tail left attached to one of the fillets
¼ cup wild rice
1½ cups fish stock (recipe, page 136) or water
¼ tsp. fennel seeds
⅛ tsp. salt
½ cup white rice
1 lb. asparagus, peeled, sliced diagonally into ¾-inch lengths and boiled for 2 minutes
2 lemons, 1 juiced, the other sliced into thin crescents
freshly ground black pepper
8 sheets phyllo dough (about 3 oz.)
1 tbsp. safflower oil
1 egg, beaten with 1 tsp. water
Red-pepper sauce
1 tbsp. virgin olive oil
1 garlic clove, crushed
2 red peppers, seeded, deribbed and coarsely chopped
½ cup fish stock (recipe, page 136) or unsalted chicken stock
½ tbsp. white wine vinegar
⅛ tsp. fennel seeds, crushed
⅛ tsp. salt
⅛ tsp. white pepper

Preheat the oven to 350° F. Put the wild rice, stock or water, fennel seeds and salt in a small, ovenproof saucepan. Bring the liquid to a boil, then cover the pan tightly, and bake the wild rice in the oven for 25 min-

utes. Stir in the white rice, return the pan to the oven and bake the mixed rice until all the liquid has been absorbed — 20 to 25 minutes more. Uncover the pan and allow the rice to cool before assembling the dish. Increase the oven temperature to 400° F.

Using tweezers or a small, sharp knife, remove any small bones from the fillets. Rinse the fillets under cold water and pat them dry. Drizzle the lemon juice over the fillets and grind some black pepper over them.

Transfer four stacked phyllo sheets to a baking sheet. Cover the remaining phyllo with a towel. Place on top of the stack the fillet that has the tail still attached, its skin side down. Spread a layer of rice over the fillet. Distribute the asparagus over the rice. Top the assembly with the second fillet, skin side up. Pat the remaining rice into the form of a fish head. Wrap the stacked phyllo around the trout and tuck the corners under the fish. Brush the entire assembly with the safflower oil.

Cut the remaining phyllo sheets into 10 strips, each 12 inches long and 4 inches wide. Fold each strip lengthwise into thirds. Lay a folded strip crosswise over the fish and tuck both ends under the bottom. Repeat the process with the remaining strips, overlapping them in evenly spaced ribbons from head to tail. With scissors, snip one edge of each ribbon at ½-inch intervals. Brush the ribbons lightly with the beaten egg.

Bake the fish until the pastry ribbons turn golden brown — about 25 minutes.

Meanwhile, prepare the sauce. Heat the olive oil in a large skillet over medium heat. Add the garlic and cook it for one minute, then add the peppers and cook them until they are soft — about two minutes more. Pour in the stock and vinegar, then stir in the fennel seeds, salt and white pepper. When the mixture simmers, remove it from the heat. Purée the mixture and strain it through a fine sieve into a sauceboat.

Transfer the fish to a serving platter and garnish it with the lemon slices on top. Let the fish cool for five minutes before slicing it. Serve the sauce alongside.

SUGGESTED ACCOMPANIMENT: *sliced fresh fennel.*

Ocean Perch Creole

Serves 6
Working time: about 20 minutes
Total time: about 30 minutes

Calories **218**
Protein **21g.**
Cholesterol **65mg.**
Total fat **9g.**
Saturated fat **3g.**
Sodium **370mg.**

1 ¼ lb. ocean perch fillets (or red snapper or striped bass), the skin left on, cut into 6 equal pieces
1 ½ tbsp. unsalted butter
1 small onion, coarsely chopped
1 green pepper, seeded, deribbed and coarsely chopped
1 garlic clove, finely chopped
1 ½ lb. ripe tomatoes, peeled, seeded and coarsely chopped, or 14 oz. canned unsalted whole tomatoes, drained and coarsely chopped
½ cup fish stock (recipe, page 136) or water
1 cup thinly sliced okra
3 tbsp. Dijon mustard
2 tbsp. paprika, preferably Hungarian
½ tsp. salt
freshly ground black pepper
¼ lb. small shrimp, peeled and deveined
½ cup flour
2 tbsp. safflower oil

To prepare the sauce, first melt the butter in a saucepan over medium heat. Add the onion and green pepper; cook, stirring occasionally, until the onion becomes transparent and begins to turn golden — four to five minutes. Add the garlic and cook it, stirring, for 30 seconds. Stir in the tomatoes, stock or water, okra, mustard, paprika, ¼ teaspoon of the salt and some black pepper. Bring the mixture to a boil, reduce the heat to medium low and simmer the sauce for five minutes. Stir in the shrimp and cook the sauce for one minute more. Set the saucepan aside.

Rinse the fillets under cold running water and pat them dry with paper towels. Season the fillets with the remaining ¼ teaspoon of salt and some black pepper. Place the fish in a paper bag with the flour and shake the bag to coat the fillets.

Heat the oil in a large, heavy-bottomed skillet over medium-high heat. Sauté the fillets in the oil until they are opaque all the way through — approximately two minutes per side. Reheat the tomato sauce and pour it into a serving platter. Lay the fillets on top of the sauce and serve.

SUGGESTED ACCOMPANIMENT: *corn-bread muffins.*

Almond-Sprinkled Mahimahi Stuffed with Chilies and Tomatoes

THE COLORFUL DOLPHIN CALLED MAHIMAHI — A FISH, NOT A MAMMAL — IS CAUGHT IN SEMITROPICAL WATERS ON BOTH COASTS OF NORTH AMERICA.

Serves 6
Working time: about 40 minutes
Total time: about 1 hour

Calories **260**	1½ lb. mahimahi fillet (or sea trout)
Protein **25g.**	2 tbsp. virgin olive oil
Cholesterol **103mg.**	3 garlic cloves, thinly sliced
Total fat **14g.**	1 or 2 small chili peppers, seeded and finely chopped (caution, page 41)
Saturated fat **3g.**	1 red onion, thinly sliced
Sodium **300mg.**	1 lb. ripe tomatoes, peeled, seeded and chopped
	2 lemons
	½ tsp. salt
	¾ cup coarsely chopped fresh parsley
	1 tbsp. unsalted butter
	½ cup sliced almonds

Rinse the fillet under cold running water and pat it dry with paper towels. With a sharp, thin-bladed knife, cut a large flap on one side of the center line of the fillet: Holding the knife parallel to the center line at a flat angle, use short slicing strokes to cut from the middle toward the edge of the fillet. (Take care not to cut all the way through to the edge nor down to the bottom of the fillet.) Repeat the process to cut a flap on the other side of the center line. Set the fish aside.

Preheat the oven to 475° F.

To prepare the stuffing, first pour the oil into a large, heavy-bottomed skillet over medium-high heat. Add the garlic and chili peppers and cook them for 30 seconds. Stir in the onion and cook for two minutes more. Add the tomatoes, the juice of one of the lemons and ¼ teaspoon of the salt. Cook the mixture, stirring often, until the tomatoes are very soft and almost all the liquid has evaporated — about 10 minutes.

While the stuffing mixture is cooking, cut six paper-thin slices from the remaining lemon and set them aside. Rub the juice from the remainder of the lemon over the outside of the fish and inside the flaps as well. Put the fish in a lightly oiled baking dish.

Stir the parsley into the tomato stuffing. Open the flaps on the fillet and fill the pocket with the stuffing. Close over the flaps and arrange the lemon slices in a decorative pattern on top of the stuffing. Bake the fish until it is opaque and feels firm to the touch — 20 to 25 minutes.

Just before the fish is done, melt the butter in a small skillet over medium heat. Add the almonds and the remaining ¼ teaspoon of salt; toast the almonds, stirring constantly, until they are lightly browned — two to

three minutes. Remove the pan from the heat. Carefully transfer the baked fish to a serving platter and scatter the almonds over the top. Serve immediately.

SUGGESTED ACCOMPANIMENT: *steamed rice.*

Oven-Steamed Rockfish

Serves 6
Working time: about 10 minutes
Total time: about 50 minutes

Calories **120**
Protein **21g.**
Cholesterol **42mg.**
Total fat **2g.**
Saturated fat **0g.**
Sodium **335mg.**

one 3-lb. whole rockfish (or black sea bass or ocean perch), cleaned and scaled
2 tbsp. dry sherry
2 tsp. cornstarch
⅛ tsp. salt
one 2-inch piece of fresh ginger, peeled and julienned
4 scallions, trimmed and cut into 2-inch-long pieces
¼ cup loosely packed cilantro leaves
2 tbsp. low-sodium soy sauce
1 tbsp. Chinese black vinegar or balsamic vinegar
¼ tsp. sugar

Combine the sherry, cornstarch and salt in a small bowl. Rinse the fish under cold running water and pat it dry with paper towels. Cut four or five diagonal slashes on each side of the fish. Rub the sherry marinade over the fish, inside and out, working some of it into the slashes. Place the fish on the shiny side of a large piece of aluminum foil and let it marinate for at least 15 minutes.

Preheat the oven to 450° F. Insert a strip of ginger and a piece of scallion into each of the slashes on the fish. Place the remaining ginger and scallions in the body cavity. Lay a few cilantro leaves on the outside of the fish; put the remaining leaves in the cavity.

Combine the soy sauce, vinegar and sugar, and pour the mixture over the fish. Fold the foil over the fish and crimp the edges to seal the package tightly.

Set the foil package on a baking sheet and bake the fish until its flesh is opaque and feels firm to the touch — about 25 minutes. Carefully transfer the fish to a warmed serving platter. Pour over the fish any liquid that has collected in the foil during baking, and serve immediately.

SUGGESTED ACCOMPANIMENTS: *stir-fried broccoli and water chestnuts; steamed rice.*

Grilled Swordfish
with Ancho Chili Sauce

Serves 6
Working time: about 30 minutes
Total time: about 1 hour

Calories **265**
Protein **28g.**
Cholesterol **56mg.**
Total fat **9g.**
Saturated fat **1g.**
Sodium **325mg.**

6 small swordfish steaks (about 5 oz. each), ½ to ¾ inch thick
2 tbsp. fresh thyme, or 2 tsp. dried thyme leaves
3 garlic cloves, finely chopped
juice of 2 lemons
4 dried ancho chili peppers, stemmed and seeded (caution, page 41)
1 oz. sun-dried tomatoes (3 or 4)
¾ cup fish stock (recipe, page 136)
½ cup tawny port
2 tsp. safflower oil

Rinse the steaks under cold running water and pat them dry with paper towels. In a shallow dish large enough to hold the steaks in a single layer, combine the thyme, two thirds of the garlic and the lemon juice. Put the steaks in the dish and marinate them in the refrigerator for one hour, turning them once or twice.

Start the coals in an outdoor grill about 40 minutes before serving time. While the coals are heating, cover the chilies with 1 quart of boiling water and soak them for 20 minutes.

Drain the chilies and transfer them to a blender or food processor. Add the tomatoes and stock, and purée the mixture.

Pour the port into a nonreactive saucepan over medium-high heat; bring the port to a boil and cook it

until it is reduced by half — three to four minutes. Stir in the chili-tomato purée and the remaining third of the garlic. Reduce the heat to medium and cook the sauce, stirring occasionally, for five minutes. Strain the sauce through a fine sieve into the bottom of a warmed serving platter.

When the coals are hot, remove the steaks from the marinade and brush them with the oil. Grill the steaks for only two or three minutes per side — the flesh should be barely opaque. Set the steaks on top of the sauce and serve immediately.

SUGGESTED ACCOMPANIMENTS: *green salad; corn bread.*
EDITOR'S NOTE: *If you wish to broil rather than grill the steaks, cook them for just two to three minutes per side.*

Grilled Swordfish
in Apple-Tarragon Sauce

Serves 4
Working time: about 15 minutes
Total time: about 25 minutes

Calories **304**
Protein **30g.**
Cholesterol **59mg.**
Total fat **10g.**
Saturated fat **2g.**
Sodium **290mg.**

1½ lb. swordfish steak (or shark or tuna), trimmed and cut into quarters
2 tbsp. safflower oil
2 tbsp. finely chopped shallot
2 tbsp. chopped fresh tarragon, or 2 tsp. dried tarragon
½ cup fish stock (recipe, page 136)
¼ cup unsweetened apple juice
1½ tsp. cornstarch, mixed with 1 tbsp. cold water
¼ tsp. salt
freshly ground black pepper
1 red apple, quartered, cored and cut into thin wedges
1 yellow apple, quartered, cored and cut into thin wedges

Preheat the grill or broiler.

To prepare the sauce, pour 1 tablespoon of the oil into a saucepan over medium heat. Add the shallot and cook it until it is translucent — one to two minutes. Add the tarragon, stock, apple juice, cornstarch mixture, ⅛ teaspoon of the salt and some pepper. Whisking constantly, bring the mixture to a boil and let it thicken. Reduce the heat to low and simmer the sauce for two or three minutes. Set the pan aside.

Rinse the fish steaks under cold running water and pat them dry with paper towels. Season the steaks with the remaining ⅛ teaspoon of salt and a generous grinding of pepper, then brush them with the remaining tablespoon of oil. Grill or broil the steaks until their flesh is opaque and feels firm to the touch — three to four minutes per side.

When the fish is nearly done, reheat the sauce over low heat. Serve the steaks immediately, topped with the warm sauce and garnished with the apple slices.

SUGGESTED ACCOMPANIMENT: *sautéed yellow squash.*

Catfish Gratin

Serves 6
Working time: about 40 minutes
Total time: about 1 hour and 10 minutes

Calories **300**
Protein **19g.**
Cholesterol **47mg.**
Total fat **9g.**
Saturated fat **3g.**
Sodium **170mg.**

1 lb. skinned catfish fillets (techniques, pages 129, 130)
juice of 1 lemon
freshly ground black pepper
2 lb. boiling potatoes, scrubbed
2½ lb. ripe tomatoes, quartered, or 28 oz. canned unsalted whole tomatoes, chopped, the juice reserved
1 jalapeño pepper, seeded and chopped (caution, page 41)
2 garlic cloves, finely chopped
1 tsp. chopped fresh oregano, or ½ tsp. dried oregano
¼ tsp. ground cumin
¼ tsp. cayenne pepper
¼ tsp. salt
1 tbsp. virgin olive oil
2 onions, thinly sliced

Herbed topping

½ cup dry bread crumbs
2 tbsp. chopped fresh parsley
¼ tsp. chopped fresh oregano, or ⅛ tsp. dried oregano
⅛ tsp. ground cumin
1½ tbsp. unsalted butter

Rinse the catfish fillets under cold running water and pat them dry with paper towels. Put them on a plate and drizzle the lemon juice over them. Season the fillets with a liberal grinding of black pepper and set them aside while you prepare the potatoes.

Put the potatoes in a saucepan, pour in enough water to cover them by about 1 inch and bring the water to a boil. Reduce the heat to medium and cook the potatoes until they are tender when pierced with a fork — about 20 minutes.

While the potatoes are cooking, prepare the sauce. Put the fresh tomatoes in a large skillet with ½ cup of water. (If you are using canned tomatoes, add their juice but no water.) Cook the tomatoes over medium heat, stirring frequently, until they are very soft and most of the liquid has evaporated — about 20 minutes. Purée the tomatoes in a food mill or work them through a sieve. Combine the tomato purée with the jalapeño pepper, garlic, oregano, cumin, cayenne pepper and salt.

Heat the oil in a large, heavy-bottomed skillet over medium-high heat. Add the onions and cook them, stirring constantly, until they are golden brown and quite soft — about seven minutes. Add ½ cup of water to the onions to deglaze the pan; stir well and set the pan aside.

Preheat the oven to 450° F. When the potatoes are cool enough to handle, peel them and cut them into chunks. In a large baking dish, mix the potatoes with the tomato sauce and the onions. Carefully place the fillets on top of the potato mixture.

To prepare the topping, combine the bread crumbs, parsley, oregano and cumin. Sprinkle the topping over the fillets, covering them completely. Cut the butter into small pieces and scatter them over the topping. Bake the dish until the fish feels firm to the touch — 15 to 20 minutes, depending on the fillets' thickness.

SUGGESTED ACCOMPANIMENT: *spinach salad.*

Skate with Red Pepper and Green Beans

Serves 4
Working (and total) time: about 40 minutes

Calories **325**
Protein **31g.**
Cholesterol **61mg.**
Total fat **10g.**
Saturated fat **1g.**
Sodium **275mg.**

2 lb. skate wings (or ray), skinned
2 cups dry white wine
1 cup fish stock (recipe, page 136) or water
1 shallot, thinly sliced
2 fresh thyme sprigs, or ¾ tsp. dried thyme leaves
8 whole cloves
4 scallions, trimmed and thinly sliced, the white parts kept separate from the green
¼ cup red wine vinegar
2 tbsp. virgin olive oil
1 tbsp. fresh lemon juice
1 red pepper, seeded, deribbed and thinly sliced
¼ tsp. salt
freshly ground black pepper
5 oz. green beans, trimmed, halved lengthwise diagonally

Rinse the skate well under cold running water. In a large, nonreactive skillet, combine the wine, the stock or water, the shallot, thyme and cloves. Bring the mixture to a boil, then reduce the heat to medium low and put the skate in the liquid. Poach the fish until it is opaque — about 12 minutes.

While the skate is cooking, prepare the vinaigrette: Combine the white scallion parts, the vinegar, oil and lemon juice in a large bowl. Set the vinaigrette aside.

When the skate is cooked, transfer it to a plate. Strain the poaching liquid into a bowl, then pour the strained liquid back into the skillet. Add the pepper strips, the salt and some pepper, and cook over medium-low heat for five minutes. Add the beans to the skillet; cook the vegetables for five minutes more.

With a slotted spoon, transfer the vegetables to the bowl containing the vinaigrette. Stir the green scallion parts into the vegetable mixture. Increase the heat un-der the skillet to high and cook the liquid rapidly until it is syrupy — two to three minutes. Pour the liquid into the vegetable mixture.

With your fingers, lift the skate meat from the cartilage. Put the meat on a serving platter and arrange the vegetables around it, spooning some of the vinaigrette over the top. Serve warm or cold.

EDITOR'S NOTE: *If the skate wings have not been skinned beforehand, slip a sharp, thin-bladed knife between the skin and the flesh. Pressing the knife against the flesh and working toward the edge of the wing, cut away the skin with short slicing strokes. Turn the wing over and repeat the process to remove the skin from the other side.*

Red Snapper in Saffron Sauce

Serves 4
Working (and total) time: about 30 minutes

Calories **240**
Protein **24g.**
Cholesterol **63mg.**
Total fat **7g.**
Saturated fat **4g.**
Sodium **270mg.**

1 lb. skinned red snapper fillets (or grouper)
¼ tsp. salt
1 cup dry white wine
1 shallot, chopped
1 garlic clove, crushed
1 fresh thyme sprig, or ½ tsp. dried thyme leaves
1 tsp. fennel seeds, crushed
10 black peppercorns, cracked
1 tbsp. unsalted butter
20 saffron threads, steeped in ¼ cup hot water for 10 minutes
1 tsp. Dijon mustard
¼ cup light cream, mixed with ½ tsp. cornstarch

Gently rinse the fillets under cold running water and pat them dry with paper towels. Sprinkle the fish with the salt and set it aside.

In a large, heavy-bottomed skillet, combine the wine, shallot, garlic, thyme, fennel seeds, peppercorns and butter. Bring the mixture to a boil, then reduce the heat to medium and simmer for three minutes. Put the fillets in the liquid and reduce the heat to low. Cover the pan and poach the fish until it is opaque and feels firm to the touch — about six minutes. Carefully transfer the fish to a warmed serving dish and cover the fish with aluminum foil to keep it warm.

Increase the heat under the skillet to medium high and reduce the poaching liquid to approximately ½ cup — about five minutes. Strain the liquid into a small saucepan. Pour into the saucepan any juices that have collected on the serving dish, then stir in the saffron mixture and the mustard. Simmer the sauce for two minutes. Whisk in the cream-and-cornstarch mixture, and cook the sauce until it thickens slightly — about one minute more. Pour the sauce around the fillets and serve at once.

SUGGESTED ACCOMPANIMENT: *boiled red potatoes.*

Stir-Fried Shark
with Nappa Cabbage

Serves 4
Working time: about 15 minutes
Total time: about 30 minutes

Calories **240**
Protein **25g.**
Cholesterol **44mg.**
Total fat **9g.**
Saturated fat **1g.**
Sodium **355mg.**

1 lb. shark meat (or swordfish or tuna)
2 tbsp. low-sodium soy sauce
1 tbsp. dark sesame oil
1 tbsp. fresh lime juice
1 bunch scallions, trimmed, sliced diagonally into ½-inch pieces, the white parts kept separate from the green
2 garlic cloves, finely chopped
1 tbsp. orange marmalade or apricot preserves
freshly ground black pepper
1½ tbsp. safflower oil
1 carrot, peeled, halved lengthwise and cut diagonally into thin slices
1 small Nappa cabbage (about 1 lb.), trimmed and sliced into ¾-inch-wide strips

Wash the shark meat under cold running water and pat it dry with paper towels. Cut it into pieces about 2 inches long and ½ inch wide. In a large bowl, combine 1 tablespoon of the soy sauce with the sesame oil, lime juice, white scallion parts, garlic, marmalade or preserves and some pepper. Add the fish pieces to the mixture and let them marinate for at least 15 minutes.

In a wok or a large skillet, heat 1 tablespoon of the safflower oil over high heat. Add the carrot slices and stir fry them for one minute, then add the cabbage, all but 1 tablespoon of the green scallion parts and the remaining tablespoon of soy sauce. Stir fry the vegetables until the cabbage is barely wilted — about two minutes. Transfer the vegetables to a bowl.

Heat the remaining ½ tablespoon of safflower oil in the wok or skillet over high heat. Add the marinated fish and gently stir fry it until it is opaque and feels firm to the touch — approximately two minutes. Return the vegetables to the pan and toss them with the shark. Transfer the mixture to a large plate, sprinkle with the reserved 1 tablespoon green scallion parts, and serve.

SUGGESTED ACCOMPANIMENT: *fresh Asian egg noodles.*

Prosciutto-Stuffed Flounder Fillets with Hot-and-Sour Sauce

Serves 4
Working time: about 30 minutes
Total time: about 1 hour

Calories **145**
Protein **21g.**
Cholesterol **57mg.**
Total fat **3g.**
Saturated fat **1g.**
Sodium **345mg.**

4 flounder or sole fillets (about 4 oz. each)
2 tbsp. rice wine or dry white wine
4 scallions, trimmed, the bottom 3 inches halved lengthwise, the tops thinly sliced diagonally
8 snow peas, strings removed and halved lengthwise
½ red pepper, seeded, deribbed and cut lengthwise into thin strips
1 paper-thin slice of prosciutto or other dry-cured ham (about ½ oz.), cut into 8 thin strips

Hot-and-sour sauce

1 lemon
1 tbsp. rice vinegar
1 tbsp. low-sodium soy sauce
1 tsp. sweet chili sauce, or ½ tsp. crushed red pepper mixed with 1 tsp. corn syrup and ½ tsp. vinegar
¼ tsp. dark sesame oil
1 tsp. cornstarch, mixed with 2 tsp. water
1 tsp. safflower oil
1 tbsp. grated fresh ginger
1 garlic clove, finely chopped

Rinse the fillets under cold running water and pat them dry with paper towels. Put the fillets in a shallow dish and sprinkle them with the wine; let the fish marinate in the refrigerator for 30 minutes.

At the end of the marinating time, blanch the scallion bottoms and snow peas together in boiling water

for 10 seconds. (The pepper strips do not require blanching.) Drain the scallions and snow peas and refresh them under cold running water. Drain the wine from the fillets and discard it; pat the fillets dry.

Lay one fourth of the scallion bottoms, snow peas and red pepper and two strips of prosciutto across the center of a fillet. Roll up the fillet and place it seam side down on a plate. Roll up the remaining fillets and vegetables and set each roll on the plate. Set the plate in a bamboo steamer basket and put the basket in a wok or large skillet filled 1 inch deep with water. (If you lack such a steamer, set the plate atop a flat wire rack in the bottom of a large saucepan or skillet filled about ½ inch deep with water.) Cover tightly and steam the fish rolls until their flesh is opaque — about six minutes.

Meanwhile, make the hot-and-sour sauce. Grate the zest of the lemon into a small bowl. Squeeze the lemon juice into the bowl and add the vinegar, soy sauce, sweet chili sauce, dark sesame oil and cornstarch. Stir the mixture thoroughly. Heat the safflower oil in a small, heavy-bottomed skillet over medium heat. Add the ginger and garlic and cook them for two minutes, taking care not to let the garlic brown. Stir in the vinegar mixture and cook the sauce for about one minute to thicken it slightly.

When the fish rolls are done, drain the accumulated liquid on the plate into the sauce; stir the sauce well to incorporate the liquid. Carefully transfer the fish rolls to individual plates. Pour the sauce over them and garnish them with the sliced scallion tops. Serve the fish rolls immediately.

SUGGESTED ACCOMPANIMENT: *cellophane noodles tossed with dark sesame oil.*

Halibut Steaks in Peppery Papaya Sauce

Serves 4
Working time: about 25 minutes
Total time: about 40 minutes

Calories **275**
Protein **28g.**
Cholesterol **81mg.**
Total fat **13g.**
Saturated fat **5g.**
Sodium **240mg.**

1½ lb. halibut (or mahimahi), cut into 4 steaks
1 tbsp. safflower oil
1 papaya (about 1 lb.), peeled, seeded and cut into 1-inch pieces
1 small onion, coarsely chopped
¼ tsp. salt
½ cup fish stock (recipe, page 136)
⅓ cup fresh lime juice
3 tbsp. heavy cream
½ dried ancho chili pepper, seeded and sliced into paper-thin strips, (caution, page 41), or ¾ tsp. crushed red pepper
2 scallions, trimmed and sliced diagonally into ½-inch pieces

Heat the oil in a large, nonreactive skillet over medium heat. Add the papaya, onion and ⅛ teaspoon of the salt. Cook the mixture, stirring frequently, for seven minutes. Pour in the stock and all but 1 tablespoon of the lime juice. Bring the liquid to a boil, reduce the heat to low, and simmer the mixture, partially covered, for 10 minutes.

Preheat the broiler.

Transfer the papaya mixture to a food processor or blender. Purée the mixture until it is smooth, stopping once to scrape down the sides. Put the cream and the chili pepper or crushed red pepper in a nonreactive saucepan over medium heat. Simmer the cream for three minutes, whisking occasionally. Reduce the heat to low and whisk the papaya purée into the cream a spoonful at a time.

Rinse the steaks under cold running water and pat them dry with paper towels. Sprinkle the fish with the remaining ⅛ teaspoon of salt and the remaining tablespoon of lime juice. Put the steaks in a lightly-buttered shallow, flameproof dish and broil them about 4 inches below the heat source for four minutes on the first side. Turn them over, sprinkle them with the sliced scallions, and continue cooking until the flesh feels firm to the touch and the scallions are browned — approximately three minutes.

Transfer the steaks to a warmed platter and spoon the papaya sauce around them. Serve immediately.

SUGGESTED ACCOMPANIMENT: *rice salad.*

Seviche of Flounder

SEVICHE IS A SPANISH WORD FOR RAW FISH "COOKED" IN AN ACIDIC MARINADE. SO THAT THE FISH WILL BE THE FRESHEST POSSIBLE, THE BONING AND FILLETING SHOULD BE DONE JUST BEFORE THE DISH IS ASSEMBLED.

Serves 6 as an appetizer
Working time: about 30 minutes
Total time: about 3 hours and 30 minutes

Calories **110**
Protein **15g.**
Cholesterol **41mg.**
Total fat **1g.**
Saturated fat **0g.**
Sodium **170mg.**

one 3-lb. whole flounder (or sole), boned and filleted, yielding about 1 lb. of fillets
4 lemons, halved and juiced, the juice and 6 of the empty halves reserved
juice of 5 limes
½ cup fresh orange juice
3 hot chili peppers (preferably serrano), halved, seeded and thinly sliced crosswise (caution, page 41)
2 tbsp. chopped cilantro or fresh parsley
1 garlic clove, finely chopped
2 tbsp. sugar
¼ tsp. salt
freshly ground black pepper
18 lettuce leaves (preferably Boston), washed and dried
1 small red onion, thinly sliced, the rings separated

Rinse the fillets under cold running water and pat them dry with paper towels. Cut the fillets into bite-size strips about 2½ inches long and 1 inch wide; then arrange the fish strips in a single layer in a shallow 8-by-11-inch glass dish.

In a separate bowl, combine all of the remaining ingredients except the reserved lemon halves, the lettuce and onion. Stir the mixture well and pour it over the fish. If the liquid does not just cover the fish, add more lemon juice until it does. Cover the dish and refrigerate it until the thickest piece of fish, when cut in half, is opaque throughout — about three hours.

Cut the edge of each reserved lemon half in a decorative sawtooth pattern. To serve the seviche, spoon some of it into each lemon half. Divide the lettuce among six serving plates. Set a filled lemon half and some of the remaining seviche atop the lettuce on each plate, and garnish with the onion rings.

Sole Baked in Parchment

Serves 4
Working time: about 15 minutes
Total time: about 30 minutes

Calories **170**
Protein **20g.**
Cholesterol **70mg.**
Total fat **8g.**
Saturated fat **4g.**
Sodium **275mg.**

4 sole or flounder fillets, about 4 oz. each
1 small zucchini, thinly sliced
1 small yellow squash, thinly sliced
3 large mushrooms, thinly sliced
4 fresh thyme sprigs, or ½ tsp. dried thyme leaves
¼ cup dry vermouth or dry white wine
2 tbsp. unsalted butter, cut into small pieces
¼ tsp. salt
freshly ground black pepper

Preheat the oven to 425° F. Rinse the fillets under cold running water and pat them dry with paper towels. Using a diagonal lengthwise cut, divide each fillet in half to make one thick fillet and one thin one.

Cut four pieces of parchment paper or aluminum foil about 12 inches by 18 inches. Fold each piece in half lengthwise, then cut each piece into a half-heart shape, as you would a valentine. Flatten out and lightly butter each heart.

Layer one fourth of the fish and vegetables on one half of a heart. Begin with a bed of zucchini and yellow squash (but save enough of both to form a top layer). Place a thick fillet on the squash bed; top the fillet with the mushrooms. Put a thin fillet on top of the mushrooms, and top it in turn with a final layer of the reserved squash. To each layered assembly, add a sprig of fresh thyme or a sprinkling of dried thyme, 1 tablespoon of the vermouth or wine, one fourth of the butter, one fourth of the salt and some pepper.

Fold the other half of the heart over the layered assembly and bring the cut edges together. Seal the package by crimping the cut edges together in a series of small, neat folds.

Transfer the packages to a baking sheet. Bake them for 10 minutes per inch of thickness of the entire assembly — approximately 15 minutes in all.

Put the packages on individual plates; let each diner open his own package.

SUGGESTED ACCOMPANIMENT: *pita bread.*

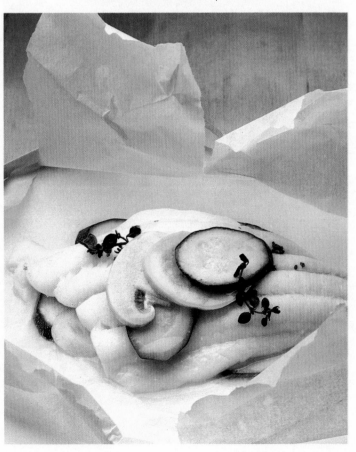

Flounder-Stuffed Tomatoes

Serves 6 as an appetizer
Working time: about 35 minutes
Total time: about 45 minutes

Calories **155**
Protein **15g.**
Cholesterol **43mg.**
Total fat **7g.**
Saturated fat **2g.**
Sodium **200mg.**

1 lb. flounder fillets (or halibut or sole)
6 ripe tomatoes
3 carrots, peeled and thinly sliced
2 tbsp. fresh lemon juice
1½ tbsp. virgin olive oil
5 garlic cloves, crushed
1 large shallot, chopped
1 tsp. fresh thyme, or ¼ tsp. dried thyme leaves
¼ tsp. salt
freshly ground black pepper
¼ cup light cream

Rinse the fillets under cold running water and pat them dry with paper towels. Slice the fillets crosswise into pieces about ½ inch wide.

Slice the tops off the tomatoes and reserve them. With a spoon, scoop out and discard the seeds and pulp. Set the tomatoes upside down on paper towels to drain. Preheat the oven to 400° F.

Cook the carrots in boiling water with the lemon juice until they are quite soft — about 15 minutes.

While the carrots are cooking, heat the oil in a large, heavy-bottomed skillet over medium heat. Add the garlic cloves and cook them for two minutes. Stir in the shallot and cook it for 30 seconds. Add the fish pieces, the thyme, ⅛ teaspoon of the salt and a generous grinding of pepper. Cook the mixture for 10 minutes, stirring gently with a fork to break up the fish. Stir in the cream and remove the skillet from the heat. Discard the cloves of garlic.

When the carrots are done, drain them, reserving ⅓ cup of the cooking liquid. In a food processor, blender or food mill, purée the carrots, reserved cooking liquid, the remaining ⅛ teaspoon of salt and some pepper until smooth. Add the carrot purée to the skillet and mix gently; spoon the mixture into the tomato shells.

Put the filled tomato shells on a cookie sheet or in a baking dish and cover them with the reserved tops. Bake the shells until their skin starts to crack — about 10 minutes. Remove the shells from the oven and discard the tops. Serve at once.

Petrale Sole with Curried Tomato Sauce

PETRALE SOLE, A LARGE PACIFIC FLOUNDER, IS PRIZED FOR THE FIRM TEXTURE OF ITS FLESH.

Serves 4
Working time: about 20 minutes
Total time: about 50 minutes

Calories **195**
Protein **23g.**
Cholesterol **57mg.**
Total fat **6g.**
Saturated fat **1g.**
Sodium **215mg.**

1 lb. petrale or gray sole fillets, rinsed and patted dry
1 shallot, finely chopped
1 garlic clove, finely chopped
⅛ tsp. salt
freshly ground black pepper
1 tbsp. dry white wine
⅓ cup fish stock (recipe, page 136) or water
parsley sprigs
Curried tomato sauce
1 tbsp. virgin olive oil
2 garlic cloves, finely chopped
2 tsp. curry powder
2½ lb. ripe tomatoes, peeled, seeded and finely chopped
⅛ tsp. salt
freshly ground black pepper
2 tsp. tomato paste
1 tbsp. chopped fresh parsley

To make the sauce, heat the oil in a large, heavy-bottomed saucepan over low heat. Add the garlic and stir until it is soft but not browned — about 30 seconds. Sprinkle in the curry powder and cook for 30 seconds more, stirring constantly. Stir in the tomatoes, salt and some pepper, and simmer until the tomatoes are very soft — about 30 minutes. Add the tomato paste, then purée the sauce, return it to the pan, and set it aside.

Preheat the oven to 425° F. Lightly oil the bottom of a heavy, shallow baking dish. Cut a piece of parchment paper or aluminum foil to the dimensions of the dish, and lightly oil one side of it. Set it aside.

Sprinkle the chopped shallot and garlic into the baking dish. Fold the fillets in half, arrange them in the dish and sprinkle them with the salt and some pepper. Pour the wine and the stock or water over the fish. Lay the parchment paper or foil, oiled side down, over the fish. Bake the fillets until their flesh is opaque — approximately nine minutes.

Remove the parchment paper or foil and set it aside. With two slotted spatulas, carefully transfer the fillets to a warmed serving platter. Re-cover the fillets with the parchment paper or foil and keep them warm. Strain the cooking liquid through a fine sieve into the reserved tomato sauce. Bring the sauce to a boil and cook it, stirring, until it thickens — about two minutes. Stir in the chopped parsley.

Spoon the sauce around the fish fillets and garnish them with the parsley sprigs. Serve immediately, with the remaining sauce on the side.

SUGGESTED ACCOMPANIMENT: *julienned zucchini.*

Shrimp and Asparagus Wrapped in Sole

Serves 6
Working (and total) time: about 1 hour

Calories **200**	*3 sole or flounders, about 1¼ lb. to 1½ lb. each*
Protein **21g.**	*1½ cups dry white wine*
Cholesterol **92mg.**	*1 tbsp. red wine vinegar*
Total fat **5g.**	*½ lb. medium shrimp, peeled and deveined, the*
Saturated fat **2g.**	*shells reserved*
Sodium **125mg.**	*⅓ lb. asparagus, sliced diagonally into ¼-inch pieces*
	2 tbsp. finely cut fresh dill
	3 shallots, finely chopped
	1½ tbsp. fresh lemon juice
	freshly ground black pepper
	3 ripe tomatoes, peeled, seeded and coarsely chopped
	2 tsp. tomato paste
	1½ tbsp. cold unsalted butter, cut into small pieces

Pour the wine, vinegar and 1 cup of water into a large, nonreactive saucepan over medium heat. Add the reserved shrimp shells and simmer them for 20 minutes to obtain an aromatic liquid.

While the shells are simmering, fillet the fish as demonstrated on page 131 (you will have six longer, thicker fillets and six shorter, thinner fillets). Rinse the fillets under cold running water, pat them dry with paper towels, and set them aside.

Strain the shrimp-shell liquid through a sieve, pushing down on the shells so that they release every bit of flavor. Discard the shells and pour the liquid back into the saucepan over medium heat. Add the shrimp and asparagus, and blanch them for 30 seconds. Remove the pan from the heat. With a slotted spoon, transfer the shrimp and asparagus to a large bowl. (Do not discard the liquid — it will serve as the base for the sauce.) Add 1 tablespoon of the dill, half of the shallots, the lemon juice and some pepper to the bowl; mix well and set the bowl aside.

Preheat the oven to 375° F. Lightly oil a baking dish. With a diagonal crosswise cut, slice one of the thinner fish fillets in half at the middle. Overlap the two halves to form a base for the assembly, and set the base in the baking dish. Wrap a larger fillet around the base to form a collar with the two ends meeting, and pin the ends together with a wooden pick. Fill the resulting shape with one sixth of the shrimp-and-asparagus mixture. Repeat the process with the remaining fillets and filling to form six portions.

Lightly cover the dish with aluminum foil, its dull side up. Bake until the sole is opaque and the shrimp and asparagus are hot — about 15 minutes.

While the fish is baking, prepare the sauce. Add the tomatoes, tomato paste and the remaining half of the shallots to the liquid in the saucepan, and set the pan over medium-high heat. Cook the sauce, stirring often, until it is reduced to about 1¼ cups — about 10 minutes. Purée the sauce in a food processor or blender. Return it to the pan and stir in the remaining tablespoon of dill. Keep the sauce warm over low heat.

When the fish is done, carefully transfer each portion to a warmed serving platter and remove the wooden picks. Whisk the butter into the sauce along with a grinding of black pepper. Pour some of the sauce around the fish and pass the rest separately.

SUGGESTED ACCOMPANIMENT: *saffron rice.*

Red Drum and Four Peppers

RED DRUM, OFTEN MARKETED AS REDFISH OR CHANNEL BASS, IS EASILY RECOGNIZED BY ITS SHINY COPPER COLOR AND THE LARGE BLACK DOT NEAR ITS TAIL.

Serves 6
Working (and total) time: about 30 minutes

Calories **210**
Protein **23g.**
Cholesterol **57mg.**
Total fat **6g.**
Saturated fat **1g.**
Sodium **275mg.**

1½ lb. skinned red drum fillet (or grouper, red snapper or tilefish)
1 tsp. chili powder
⅛ to ¼ tsp. cayenne pepper
2 tsp. dried thyme leaves
2 tbsp. virgin olive oil
½ tsp. salt
3 green peppers, seeded and deribbed, 1 pepper coarsely chopped, the remaining 2 peppers diced
2 or 3 jalapeño peppers, seeded and chopped (caution, page 41)
2 onions, chopped (about 2 cups)
3 garlic cloves, finely chopped
2 bay leaves, finely crumbled
1½ cups dry white wine
1 red pepper, seeded, deribbed and diced

Preheat the oven to 350° F.

In a small bowl, combine the chili powder, cayenne pepper and 1 teaspoon of the thyme. Rinse the fish under cold running water and pat it dry with paper towels. Slice the fish into six equal fillets; sprinkle the spice mixture evenly over the fillets.

Heat the oil in a large, heavy-bottomed skillet over medium-high heat. When the oil is hot, add the fillets and cook them on the first side for three minutes. Turn the fillets over and sprinkle them with ¼ teaspoon of the salt. Cook the fish on the second side for two minutes. Transfer the fillets to an ovenproof dish and bake them for five minutes.

Meanwhile, add the diced green peppers, the jalapeño peppers, onions, garlic, bay leaves and the remaining teaspoon of thyme to the skillet. Cook the mixture, stirring often, for five minutes. Stir in the wine, red pepper and remaining ¼ teaspoon of salt.

Remove the fish from the oven and pour into the skillet any juices that have collected in the bottom of the dish. Return the fish to the oven for five minutes more to finish baking it. Increase the heat under the skillet to high and cook the pepper mixture until most of the liquid has evaporated — about five minutes.

While the pepper mixture and fish are cooking, purée the coarsely chopped green pepper in a food processor or blender. Stir the purée into the pepper mixture in the skillet and cook it for one minute more.

Remove the fish from the oven and spoon about half of the vegetables around it. Pass the remaining vegetables in a bowl.

SUGGESTED ACCOMPANIMENT: *steamed new potatoes.*

Codfish Cakes
with Horseradish Sauce

Serves 4
Working time: about 20 minutes
Total time: about 40 minutes

Calories **180**
Protein **21g.**
Cholesterol **107mg.**
Total fat **4g.**
Saturated fat **1g.**
Sodium **490mg.**

12 oz. cod fillets (or haddock, pollock or scrod)
1 ¼ cup dry bread crumbs
1 egg
1 egg white
¾ cup finely chopped onion
¼ cup chopped Italian parsley or cilantro
3 garlic cloves, finely chopped
2 tbsp. grainy mustard
2 tbsp. anisette or other anise-flavored liqueur (optional)
2 tbsp. fresh lemon juice
1 ½ tsp. capers, drained and chopped
1 tbsp. paprika
¼ tsp. cayenne pepper
⅔ cup plain low-fat yogurt
2 tbsp. red wine vinegar
1 tsp. prepared horseradish

Preheat the oven to 400° F. With a large knife, finely chop the fish. Put the fish in a large mixing bowl. Add ½ cup of the bread crumbs, the egg, egg white, onion, all but 1 tablespoon of the parsley or cilantro, the garlic, 1 tablespoon of the mustard, the liqueur if you are using it, the lemon juice, capers, paprika and cayenne pepper, and mix thoroughly.

Put the remaining ¾ cup of bread crumbs in a shallow bowl. Divide the fish mixture into eight equal portions. Pat one of the portions into a cake about ¾ inch thick. Coat the cake well with bread crumbs and place it on an oiled baking sheet. Repeat these steps to form the remaining portions into breaded fish cakes. Bake the codfish cakes for 20 minutes.

While the cakes are in the oven, prepare the sauce. In a small bowl, mix the remaining tablespoon of the mustard and the remaining tablespoon of the parsley or cilantro with the yogurt, the vinegar and the horseradish.

Serve the cakes with a dollop of sauce on the side.

SUGGESTED ACCOMPANIMENT: *red cabbage salad.*

Baked Pollock
with Tomatoes, Zucchini and Provolone

Serves 4
Working time: about 15 minutes
Total time: about 30 minutes

Calories **215**	
Protein **27g.**	1 lb. pollock fillets (or cod or haddock)
Cholesterol **91mg.**	¼ tsp. salt
Total fat **9g.**	freshly ground black pepper
Saturated fat **3g.**	1 tbsp. virgin olive oil
Sodium **360mg.**	2 tbsp. chopped fresh basil, or 1 tbsp. dried basil
	2 garlic cloves, finely chopped
	1½ lb. ripe tomatoes, peeled, seeded and chopped, or 14 oz. canned unsalted whole tomatoes, drained, chopped and drained again
	1 small zucchini, sliced diagonally into thin ovals
	2 oz. provolone cheese, cut into thin, narrow strips

Preheat the oven to 400° F. Rinse the fillets under cold running water and pat them dry with paper towels. Sprinkle ⅛ teaspoon of the salt and some pepper over both sides of the fillets. Spread the oil in the bottom of an ovenproof casserole. Arrange the fillets in the casserole in a single layer.

Strew the basil and garlic over the fish, then cover the fish with the tomatoes. Arrange the zucchini slices in a fish-scale pattern down the center of the dish; sprinkle the remaining ⅛ teaspoon of salt over them. Cover the dish with a piece of oiled parchment paper and bake it for 10 minutes. Remove the parchment paper and place the strips of provolone in a diamond pattern around the zucchini. Cover the dish again and bake it until the fish feels firm to the touch — three to five minutes more. Serve immediately.

Haddock Enchiladas
with Tomatillo Sauce

Serves 4
Working (and total) time: about one hour

Calories **400**
Protein **23g.**
Cholesterol **50mg.**
Total fat **9g.**
Saturated fat **1g.**
Sodium **295mg.**

¾ lb. haddock fillets (or grouper or rockfish)

½ cup white rice

1 dried hot chili pepper, preferably ancho (caution, page 41), seeded and very finely chopped or ground with a mortar and pestle, or ¼ tsp. crushed red pepper

¼ tsp. salt

freshly ground black pepper

2 tbsp. safflower oil

1 garlic clove, finely chopped

1 small onion, finely chopped

1½ lb. ripe tomatoes, peeled, seeded and coarsely chopped, or 14 oz. canned unsalted whole tomatoes, drained and coarsely chopped, the juice reserved

½ cup fish stock (recipe, page 136) or white wine, or substitute the reserved juice of the chopped canned tomatoes

¼ tsp. ground cumin

8 corn tortillas

Tomatillo sauce

1 lb. fresh tomatillos, stemmed, husked and washed

1 fresh hot chili pepper (preferably serrano), seeded and chopped (caution, page 41)

2 tbsp. chopped cilantro

1 small onion, finely chopped

freshly ground black pepper

Preheat the oven to 375° F. In a 1-quart flameproof casserole, combine the rice, dried chili pepper, ⅛ teaspoon of the salt and 1¼ cups of water. Bring the liquid to a boil, then cover the casserole tightly and set it in the oven. Cook until the rice has absorbed all the liquid and is tender — about 25 minutes.

Meanwhile, make the tomatillo sauce. Put the tomatillos in a saucepan and pour in enough water to cover them. Cover the pan and set it over low heat. Gently simmer the tomatillos until they are soft — 20 to 25 minutes — then drain them and put them in a food processor or blender. Add the chili pepper, cilantro, onion and some black pepper, and blend until a coarse purée results. Set the sauce aside.

While the tomatillos are simmering, rinse the fillets

under cold running water and pat them dry with paper towels. Season the fillets on both sides with the remaining ⅛ teaspoon of salt and some black pepper.

Heat the oil in a large, heavy-bottomed skillet over medium heat. Add the garlic and cook it for 30 seconds, stirring constantly. Add the onion, the fresh tomatoes with the fish stock or wine (or the canned tomatoes with their juice), the cumin and some more black pepper. Bring the mixture to a simmer, then add the fish. Cover the skillet and simmer the contents until the fillets can be flaked at their thickest point — about seven minutes. With a fork, shred the fillets into bite-size or smaller pieces. Spoon the cooked rice over the fish mixture and stir well to combine.

To assemble the enchiladas, heat a small, heavy-bottomed skillet over medium-high heat. Place a tortilla in the skillet and warm it for 15 to 30 seconds. Turn the tortilla over and warm it on the second side for 15 to 30 seconds more. Quickly transfer the tortilla to a work surface, and lay the next tortilla in the skillet to warm. Spread ⅓ cup of the fish mixture in a line across the first tortilla, about halfway between the middle of the tortilla and the near edge. Working quickly, fold the near edge of the tortilla over the filling and roll it away from you, then place the enchilada, seam side

down, in a lightly oiled casserole. Turn the tortilla in the skillet and warm it on the second side for 15 to 30 seconds, then fill it while you warm a third tortilla. Warm and fill the remaining tortillas in the same manner and place them snugly side by side in the casserole.

Pour the tomatillo sauce over the enchiladas and warm the casserole in the oven until the enchiladas are heated through — seven to 10 minutes.

Serve the enchiladas immediately.

SUGGESTED ACCOMPANIMENT: *sautéed red and green peppers.*

Chilies — A Cautionary Note

Both dried and fresh hot chilies should be handled with care. Their flesh and seeds contain volatile oils that can make skin tingle and cause eyes to burn. Rubber gloves offer protection — but the cook should still be careful not to touch the face, lips or eyes when working with chilies.

Soaking fresh chilies in cold, salted water for an hour will remove some of their fire. If canned chilies are substituted for fresh ones, they should be rinsed in cold water in order to eliminate as much of the brine used to preserve them as possible.

Baked Cod Plaki

PLAKI IS A GREEK FISH DISH BAKED ON A BED OF TOMATOES.

Serves 6
Working time: about 30 minutes
Total time: about 45 minutes

Calories **150**
Protein **17g.**
Cholesterol **49mg.**
Total fat **5g.**
Saturated fat **3g.**
Sodium **350mg.**

1 lb. cod fillets (or haddock, halibut or pollock)
2 large ripe tomatoes, sliced
2 small onions, sliced
1 head of fennel, cored, sliced crosswise, feathery tops reserved
2 garlic cloves, finely chopped
1 tbsp. chopped fresh oregano, or 2 tsp. dried oregano
3 tbsp. dry white wine
½ cup crumbled feta cheese
2 tbsp. chopped fresh parsley
4 oil-cured black olives, pitted and sliced
freshly ground black pepper

Preheat the oven to 375° F. Lightly oil a large baking dish; layer the tomatoes, onions, fennel, garlic and oregano in the bottom. Rinse the fish under cold running water and pat it dry with paper towels. Slice the fish crosswise into pieces about 2 inches wide. Arrange the fish on top of the vegetables and sprinkle it with the wine.

Cover the dish with foil and bake the fish until it is opaque and feels firm to the touch — 15 to 20 minutes. Remove the dish from the oven. Sprinkle the fish with the feta, parsley, olives and some pepper. Garnish with some of the reserved fennel tops and serve immediately, spooning the pan juices over each portion.

SUGGESTED ACCOMPANIMENT: *lightly buttered orzo.*

Curried Grouper

Serves 4
Working time: about 15 minutes
Total time: about 25 minutes

Calories **260**
Protein **25g.**
Cholesterol **42mg.**
Total fat **8g.**
Saturated fat **1g.**
Sodium **230mg.**

1 lb. grouper fillet (or tilefish)
1 tbsp. curry powder
2 tbsp. safflower oil
3 tbsp. fresh lime juice
freshly ground black pepper
1 large red apple, cored and cut into pieces
¾ cup chopped onion
1 tsp. fennel seeds, cracked
¼ tsp. salt
1 cup peas, blanched in boiling water for 1 minute if fresh
¼ cup dry white wine

Rinse the fillet under cold running water and pat it dry with paper towels. Cut the fillet into 1-inch pieces.

In a small bowl, combine the curry powder, 1 table-spoon of the oil, the lime juice and some pepper. Put the fish pieces, apple, onion and fennel seeds into a large bowl. Pour the curry mixture over the fish and mix well. Let the fish marinate for 10 minutes.

Pour the remaining tablespoon of oil into a large, heavy-bottomed skillet over high heat. When the oil is hot, add the contents of the bowl. Sprinkle in the salt and cook the curry for three minutes, stirring constant-ly. Add the peas and white wine and continue cooking the curry, stirring often, until the fish is firm to the touch — two to three minutes more. Transfer the curry to a warmed serving dish.

SUGGESTED ACCOMPANIMENTS: *mango chutney; diced cu-cumbers; unsalted peanuts; steamed brown rice.*

Grouper with Shiitake Mushroom Sauce

Serves 4
Working (and total) time: about 35 minutes

Calories **210**
Protein **23g.**
Cholesterol **42mg.**
Total fat **8g.**
Saturated fat **1g.**
Sodium **400mg.**

one 1-lb. grouper fillet (or monkfish or red snapper)
½ oz. dried shiitake or other Asian mushrooms, soaked in ¾ cup very hot water for 20 minutes
¼ cup dry sherry
2 tbsp. low-sodium soy sauce
2 tbsp. fresh lime juice
1 tsp. sugar
1½ tsp. cornstarch
2 tbsp. safflower oil
2 scallions, trimmed and thinly sliced
1 tbsp. julienned fresh ginger
2 garlic cloves, thinly sliced
½ tsp. freshly ground black pepper

Remove the mushrooms from their soaking liquid and slice them into thin pieces. Set the mushrooms aside.

Pour ¼ cup of the soaking liquid into a mixing bowl, being careful to leave any grit from the mushrooms behind. Stir in the sherry, soy sauce, 1 tablespoon of the lime juice and the sugar. Set the mixture aside.

Rinse the fillet under cold running water and pat it dry with paper towels. Rub the fillet with the remaining tablespoon of lime juice, then rub the cornstarch evenly over both sides of the fish.

Heat the oil in a large, heavy-bottomed skillet (preferably nonstick) over high heat. When the oil is hot, add the fish and sear it on one side for two minutes. Carefully turn the fillet over and sear it on the second side for two minutes. Transfer the fish to a plate.

Add the mushrooms, scallions, ginger, garlic and pepper to the hot skillet. Cook the mixture on high for one minute, then reduce the heat to low. Pour in the sherry mixture, replace the fillet, and cover the skillet. Steam the fish until it is opaque — about five minutes. Transfer the fish to a warmed serving platter and spoon the sauce around it.

SUGGESTED ACCOMPANIMENT: *stir-fried red cabbage.*

2 *Chilled to preserve their savor, such rich-fleshed fish as bluefish, shad, pompano, butterfish and Chinook salmon tempt with plump goodness.*

The Virtues of Richness

The recipes that follow feature the so-called fatty fish — all those whose flesh has more than a 5-percent fat content. Now that such rich-fleshed fish are seen as being healthful, there is more reason than ever to enjoy them. Happily, among them are such popular species as salmon, shad, tuna, mackerel and trout. Thanks to their high concentrations of certain polyunsaturated oils, which amount to close to 15 percent in several varieties, they appear to be uniquely helpful in lowering the levels of triglycerides in humans. Indeed, the oil in fish may be one of nature's best preventives against heart disease.

Because their natural oils baste them as they cook, rich-fleshed fish respond well to broiling, grilling and baking. (Do not let this fool you: They are as easy to overcook, and therefore ruin, as the leaner fish.) The firm flesh of some varieties also makes them prime candidates for sautéing, stir frying and poaching. What could be easier to prepare — or finer to eat — than lightly sautéed salmon, served with the basil-and-shallot sauce on page 60?

Rich-fleshed fish have pronounced flavor. They may need citrus juice or wine to tame or mellow it. At the same time, they retain their identity when cooked with garlic, peppers and various other aromatic vegetables. In this section, mackerel is broiled and then set off by a rhubarb-orange sauce. Sablefish, marinated in a mixture of vinegar, lemon juice and garlic, then grilled under a coat of cracked black pepper, is served with a sauce made with the remaining marinade, fish stock, thyme and a little butter.

The rich-fleshed fish are usually caught and savored when their oil content is highest. In some parts of the country, shad is heralded as a delicacy of spring; sablefish tastes best in summer and fall. Salmon is at its most glorious just before it begins its summer spawning runs. For cooks lucky enough to catch their own rich-fleshed fish, or for those who like to buy them whole and cut them up at home, full instructions for dressing and filleting the fish appear on pages 128-130.

Spicy Broiled Shad

THE FINE ART OF BONING SHAD FILLETS IS DESCRIBED BELOW. IF
YOU PREFER, A RELIABLE FISHMONGER CAN BONE THEM FOR YOU.

Serves 6
Working time: about 30 minutes
Total time: about 1 hour

Calories **250**	2 shad fillets, about ¾ lb. each (or rainbow trout
Protein **20g.**	or salmon), the skin left on
Cholesterol **88mg.**	
Total fat **17g.**	2 tbsp. dry vermouth
Saturated fat **6g.**	juice of 1 lime
Sodium **60mg.**	juice of ½ orange
	1 jalapeño pepper, seeded and finely chopped
	(caution, page 41)
	1 garlic clove, finely chopped
	1 tsp. fresh thyme, or ¼ tsp. dried thyme leaves
	⅛ tsp. ground allspice
	1½ tbsp. unsalted butter, cut into small cubes

In a small bowl, combine the vermouth, lime juice,
orange juice, jalapeño pepper, garlic, thyme and allspice. Set the bowl aside.

Rinse the shad fillets under cold running water and
pat them dry with paper towels. To bone the fillets,
place one of them skin side down on a work surface.
With your fingers, locate the two rows of small bones;
each row lies about 1 inch on either side of the center-
line of the fillet. Using a small, sharp knife, make a long
cut on either side of one of the rows; take care not to
penetrate the skin. Working from the head end toward
the tail, gently pull the bones away in a single strip.
Repeat the process to remove the other row of bones;
bone the remaining fillet in the same manner.

Lay the fillets in an ovenproof dish and pour the
marinade over them. Let the fillets marinate for 15
minutes. Preheat the broiler.

Strain and reserve the marinade. Broil the fillets
about 3 inches below the heat source, basting them
every three minutes with the marinade, until their flesh
is opaque — 10 to 12 minutes. Scatter the cubes of
butter over the top; return the fillets to the broiler and
cook them a few seconds longer to melt the butter.
Serve immediately.

SUGGESTED ACCOMPANIMENT: *salad of tropical fruits.*

Baked Herring with Yogurt-Mint Sauce

Serves 4
Working time: about 15 minutes
Total time: about 1 hour

Calories **340**
Protein **35g.**
Cholesterol **96mg.**
Total fat **18g.**
Saturated fat **5g.**
Sodium **200mg.**

4 whole fresh herring (or mackerel), about ½ lb. each, dressed (technique, pages 128-129)
¼ cup chopped fresh mint
4 garlic cloves, finely chopped
¼ tsp. ground cumin
¼ tsp. cayenne pepper
Yogurt-mint sauce
2 tbsp. chopped fresh mint
1 cup plain low-fat yogurt
1 tbsp. virgin olive oil
3 garlic cloves, finely chopped
¼ tsp. ground cumin
¼ tsp. ground coriander
¼ tsp. ground turmeric
¼ tsp. ground cardamom (optional)
mint sprigs for garnish

Rinse the herring under cold running water and pat them dry with paper towels.

In a small bowl, combine the ¼ cup of chopped mint, the garlic, cumin and cayenne pepper. Spread one fourth of this mixture inside the cavity of each herring. Cut shallow diagonal slashes at 1-inch intervals along the sides of each fish. Lay the fish on their sides in a lightly oiled baking dish. Let the herring marinate at room temperature for 30 minutes. Preheat the oven to 500° F.

While the fish is marinating, prepare the sauce. Stir the 2 tablespoons of chopped mint into the yogurt in a bowl, and set it aside. Heat the oil in a small heavy-bottomed skillet over medium-high heat, add the garlic and cook it until it is soft — about two minutes. Stir in the cumin, coriander, turmeric and cardamom if you are using it, and cook the mixture 30 seconds. Add the spice mixture to the minted yogurt and stir well.

Bake the fish until it feels firm to the touch and is opaque throughout — about 12 minutes. Serve it immediately, accompanied by the sauce and garnished with the mint sprigs.

SUGGESTED ACCOMPANIMENT: *steamed carrots.*

Baked Whitefish with Garlic and Glazed Carrots

Serves 4
Working time: about 15 minutes
Total time: about 1 hour

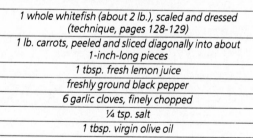

Calories **265**
Protein **23g.**
Cholesterol **54mg.**
Total fat **14g.**
Saturated fat **2g.**
Sodium **270mg.**

1 whole whitefish (about 2 lb.), scaled and dressed (technique, pages 128-129)	
1 lb. carrots, peeled and sliced diagonally into about 1-inch-long pieces	
1 tbsp. fresh lemon juice	
freshly ground black pepper	
6 garlic cloves, finely chopped	
¼ tsp. salt	
1 tbsp. virgin olive oil	

Preheat the oven to 400° F. Put the carrots in a baking dish that is large enough to accommodate the fish. Add the lemon juice, a generous grinding of pepper and one third of the chopped garlic. Pour ¾ cup of water into the dish and toss the ingredients well.

Sprinkle the fish inside and out with the salt and some pepper, and rub the remaining garlic all over it. Push the carrots to the sides of the dish and lay the fish on the bottom. Drizzle the oil over the fish. Bake, stirring the carrots every 15 minutes, until the fish is golden and the carrots are tender — about 45 minutes.

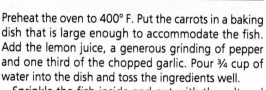

SUGGESTED ACCOMPANIMENT: *Brussels sprouts.*

Grilled Sablefish Coated with Cracked Black Pepper

Serves 6
Working time: about 35 minutes
Total time: about 4 hours and 30 minutes

Calories **290**
Protein **16g.**
Cholesterol **71mg.**
Total fat **22g.**
Saturated fat **7g.**
Sodium **200mg.**

1½ lb. sablefish (or whitefish) fillets, skinned
⅓ cup fresh lemon juice
½ cup red wine vinegar
3 garlic cloves, crushed
1½ tbsp. sugar
¼ tsp. salt
3 tbsp. black peppercorns, cracked
¾ cup fish stock (recipe, page 136) or vegetable stock
2 tsp. fresh thyme, or ½ tsp. dried thyme leaves
2 tbsp. cold unsalted butter, cut into small pieces
2 thyme sprigs for garnish

In a shallow bowl just large enough to hold the fillets in a single layer, stir together the lemon juice, vinegar, garlic, sugar and salt. Lay the fillets in the liquid, cover the bowl and let the fish marinate in the refrigerator for at least four hours; halfway through the marinating time, turn the fillets over.

Preheat the grill or broiler. Remove the fillets from the marinade and pat them dry with paper towels. Sprinkle half of the cracked pepper over the fillets and press the pepper firmly into the flesh with your fingertips. Turn the fillets over and coat them with the remaining black pepper in the same manner.

If you are grilling the fillets, place them approximately 4 inches above the heat source and cook them on the first side for six minutes. Gently turn the fillets over and cook them on the second side until their flesh just flakes — about six minutes more.

If you are broiling the fillets, cook them about 4 inches below the heat source for four to five minutes on each side.

While the fish is cooking, strain the marinade into a small nonreactive saucepan over medium heat and add the stock and thyme. Cook the mixture until it is reduced to about ½ cup — approximately five minutes. When the fillets are cooked, transfer them to a heated serving platter. Whisk the butter into the sauce, pour the sauce over the fillets, garnish with the thyme sprigs, and serve at once.

SUGGESTED ACCOMPANIMENT: *tomato salad sprinkled with chopped scallions.*

Poached Turbot
in Orange-Lemon Sauce

Serves 4
Working (and total) time: about 30 minutes

Calories **285**
Protein **16g.**
Cholesterol **68mg.**
Total fat **18g.**
Saturated fat **6g.**
Sodium **230mg.**

1 lb. turbot fillets (or flounder, halibut or sole)
¾ cup fish stock (recipe, page 136)
¾ cup dry white wine
⅔ cup fresh orange juice
1 tbsp. fresh lemon juice
2 shallots, finely chopped
1 tbsp. fresh thyme, or 1 tsp. dried thyme leaves
freshly ground black pepper
2 tbsp. unsalted butter
1 large head Boston lettuce (about 5 oz.), cored and washed
¼ tsp. salt

To prepare the poaching liquid, combine the stock, wine, orange juice, lemon juice, half of the shallots, half of the thyme and some pepper in a large, nonreactive skillet. Bring the liquid to a boil, then reduce the heat to medium low. Simmer the liquid for 10 minutes.

Rinse the fillets under cold running water and pat them dry with paper towels. Slice each fillet diagonally in half to form one thick piece and one thin piece. Place the thicker fillets in the simmering liquid and poach them gently for one minute. Add the thinner fillets and continue poaching the fish until it is opaque and feels firm to the touch — three to four minutes. Transfer the fish to a plate and keep it warm.

Raise the heat to medium and simmer the poaching liquid until it is reduced to about ½ cup. Strain the sauce through a sieve into a small pan and set it aside.

Melt 1 tablespoon of the butter in the same skillet over medium heat. Add the remaining shallots and thyme, and cook them for one minute, stirring. Add the lettuce leaves, ⅛ teaspoon of the salt and some pepper. Cook the lettuce, stirring, until it has wilted — approximately two minutes. Place the lettuce on a warmed serving plate.

Reheat the sauce; stir in the remaining ⅛ teaspoon of salt and whisk in the remaining tablespoon of butter. Put the fish pieces on the lettuce, pour the sauce over the fish and serve immediately.

SUGGESTED ACCOMPANIMENT: *steamed yellow squash with diced red pepper.*

Carp in Red Wine

Serves 6
Working time: about 40 minutes
Total time: about 1 hour and 40 minutes

Calories **335**
Protein **18g.**
Cholesterol **67mg.**
Total fat **13g.**
Saturated fat **3g.**
Sodium **160mg.**

1 whole 4½-lb. carp (or lake trout), dressed (technique, pages 128-129) and cut into 1-inch-thick steaks
2 cups pearl onions
3 cups red wine
3 cups fish stock (recipe, page 136)
3 whole cloves
1 small cinnamon stick
12 black peppercorns
¼ teaspoon salt
1 bay leaf
1 tbsp. safflower oil
½ lb. mushrooms, wiped clean, trimmed and thickly sliced
1 tsp. sugar
¼ cup golden raisins
1 tbsp. cold unsalted butter, cut into small pieces
6 chervil or parsley sprigs

Pare off the root ends of the pearl onions. Put them in a bowl and pour in enough boiling water to cover them. When the water has cooled — after about 15 minutes — remove the onions and squeeze them out of their skins. Set them aside.

In a large, heavy-bottomed skillet, combine the wine, stock, cloves, cinnamon, peppercorns, salt and bay leaf. Bring the liquid to a boil, then reduce the heat to medium and simmer the mixture for 10 minutes.

Rinse the carp steaks under cold running water. Lay the steaks in the skillet and poach them, uncovered, until the flesh is opaque and feels firm to the touch — about 10 minutes. Remove the steaks; cover them with aluminum foil and keep them warm.

Return the poaching liquid to a boil and cook it until it is reduced to 2 cups — about 15 minutes.

Meanwhile, prepare the mushrooms and onions. Pour the oil into another large, heavy-bottomed skillet over medium-high heat. When the oil is hot, add the mushrooms and sauté them until they are tender and golden — about four minutes. Use a slotted spoon to transfer the mushrooms to a bowl, and set them aside. Add the onions, sugar and 1 cup of water to the skillet. Cook the mixture until the water has evaporated and the onions are coated with a golden glaze — about seven minutes. Using the slotted spoon, transfer the onions to the bowl with the mushrooms.

Strain the reduced stock into the skillet you used to cook the onions. Add the raisins and bring the liquid to a boil. Simmer the mixture, scraping and stirring to dissolve the caramelized juices, until the liquid is reduced to about 1 cup — about five minutes. Reduce the heat to low and whisk in the butter. Add the reserved mushrooms and onions and reheat them in the sauce, then pour the sauce over the steaks. Garnish the steaks with the sprigs of chervil or parsley, and serve immediately.

SUGGESTED ACCOMPANIMENT: *steamed yellow squash.*

Salmon-Stuffed Tuna in Lettuce Leaves

Serves 6
Working time: about 30 minutes
Total time: about 40 minutes

Calories **255**
Protein **35g.**
Cholesterol **51mg.**
Total fat **10g.**
Saturated fat **2g.**
Sodium **165mg.**

2 lb. fresh tuna (or swordfish), trimmed and cut into 6 small steaks
12 lettuce leaves (red leaf or curly leaf)
2 paper-thin slices smoked salmon, each slice cut into three strips
freshly ground black pepper
1 shallot, finely chopped
2¼ cups fish stock (recipe, page 136)
3 celery stalks, julienned
2 carrots, peeled and julienned
1 large leek, trimmed, washed thoroughly to remove all grit, and julienned

Blanch the lettuce leaves in a large pot of boiling water for 10 seconds. Refresh them under cold running water. Carefully spread out the leaves — they tear easily — on a cloth. Preheat the oven to 400° F.

Lightly oil a baking dish large enough to hold the tuna steaks in a single layer. With a sharp knife, cut a pocket in the side of one of the steaks. Insert a salmon strip in the pocket, sprinkle the steak with some pepper, and wrap it in two lettuce leaves. Set the wrapped steak in the baking dish. Repeat the process to stuff and wrap the other steaks. Scatter the shallot over the steaks. Bring the stock to a boil and pour 2 cups of it over the fish. Cover the dish with aluminum foil, its shiny side down.

Put the fish in the oven; immediately reduce the heat to 350° F., and bake the fish for 15 minutes.

About five minutes before the fish finishes baking, put the celery, carrots and leek in a saucepan. Pour in the remaining ¼ cup of stock and turn the heat to medium high. Cover the pan and steam the vegetables until they are tender — three to five minutes.

Remove the dish from the oven; spoon a little of the fish-cooking liquid into the saucepan with the vegetables, then transfer the vegetables to a warmed serving platter. Carefully transfer the fish to the platter with a spatula and serve immediately.

SUGGESTED ACCOMPANIMENT: *crusty sourdough bread.*

Marinated Fresh Tuna with Peppers

Serves 6 as a first course
Working time: about 30 minutes
Total time: about 2 hours and 30 minutes

Calories **145**
Protein **15g.**
Cholesterol **23mg.**
Total fat **9g.**
Saturated fat **2g.**
Sodium **75mg.**

¾ lb. fresh tuna
2 tbsp. finely chopped red onion
¼ cup coarsely chopped fresh basil
2 tbsp. virgin olive oil
1 tbsp. fresh lemon juice
⅛ tsp. salt
freshly ground black pepper
1 red pepper
1 green pepper
1 yellow pepper

Rinse the tuna under cold running water and pat it dry with paper towels. Trim off and discard any dark red meat from the tuna. Cut the tuna into slices about ⅜ inch thick. If any slice is too thick, pound it with the heel of your hand to flatten it. Cut the slices into strips about ½ inch wide and 2 inches long.

Place the tuna strips in a shallow dish with the onion and chopped basil. In a small bowl, whisk together the oil, lemon juice, salt and pepper; pour this mixture over the tuna. With a rubber spatula, toss the tuna very gently until the strips are thoroughly coated. Cover the dish and refrigerate it for two hours, turning the tuna strips occasionally.

Preheat the broiler. Broil the peppers about 3 inches below the heat source, turning them with tongs as they blister, until their skins are blackened all over — approximately 15 minutes. Put the peppers in a large bowl and cover it tightly with plastic wrap (the trapped steam will loosen their skins). When the peppers are cool enough to handle, peel, seed and derib them. Quarter each pepper lengthwise.

To serve, arrange the marinated tuna strips and the roasted peppers on a platter.

SUGGESTED ACCOMPANIMENT: *French or Italian bread.*

EDITOR'S NOTE: *Because the tuna in this recipe is not cooked, only the freshest possible fish should be used.*

Broiled Tuna with White Beans and Red Onions

THE CLASSIC ITALIAN COMBINATION OF TUNA AND BEANS IS ENLIVENED HERE BY THE ADDITION OF PICKLED RED ONIONS.

Serves 6
Working time: about 20 minutes
Total time: about 1 day

Calories **330**
Protein **27g.**
Cholesterol **29mg.**
Total fat **13g.**
Saturated fat **2g.**
Sodium **230mg.**

1 lb. fresh tuna (or swordfish)
1 cup dried Great Northern or navy beans, soaked for at least 8 hours in water
2 garlic cloves
1 strip of lemon zest
juice of 2 lemons
½ tsp. salt
2 large red onions, thinly sliced
½ cup red wine vinegar
1 tsp. brown sugar
3 tbsp. virgin olive oil
1½ tsp. fresh thyme, or ½ tsp. dried thyme leaves
freshly ground black pepper
1 tsp. fresh rosemary, or ¼ tsp. dried rosemary
basil leaves for garnish

Drain the beans and put them in a saucepan with the garlic and lemon zest. Pour in enough cold water to cover the beans by about 1 inch. Boil the beans for 10 minutes, then reduce the heat to medium and cook them for 30 minutes. Stir in ¼ teaspoon of the salt and continue cooking the beans until they are tender — 15 to 30 minutes more.

While the beans are cooking, put the onions, vinegar and sugar in a small, nonreactive saucepan over medium-low heat. Simmer the onions, stirring them often, for 10 minutes. Transfer the onions to a small bowl and let them cool slightly, then refrigerate them.

In a mixing bowl, whisk together the lemon juice, 2 tablespoons of the oil, the remaining ¼ teaspoon of salt, half of the thyme and a generous grinding of pepper. When the beans are tender, drain them, and discard the lemon zest and garlic cloves. Add the beans to the mixing bowl and stir well.

Preheat the broiler. Rinse the tuna under cold running water and pat it dry with paper towels. Trim away any very dark red meat from the tuna. Slice the tuna into 1-inch cubes and put the cubes in a flameproof baking dish. Add the remaining tablespoon of oil, the remaining thyme, the rosemary and some pepper, and toss well to coat the tuna. Broil the tuna on the first side for two minutes. Turn the pieces over and broil them, watching that they do not overcook, until they are opaque — one or two minutes more.

Transfer the beans to a serving dish; arrange the tuna cubes on top of the beans and the pickled onions alongside. Garnish the dish with the basil leaves. Serve warm or cold.

SUGGESTED ACCOMPANIMENT: *steamed artichokes.*

Broiled Eel
in Ginger-Sherry Sauce
on Rice Fingers

Serves 4 as a first course
Working time: about 30 minutes
Total time: about 40 minutes

Calories **420**
Protein **20g.**
Cholesterol **93mg.**
Total fat **14g.**
Saturated fat **3g.**
Sodium **370mg.**

1 lb. eel
1 tsp. rice vinegar
1 cup glutinous rice, preferably sushi rice
1 tsp. wasabi (Japanese horseradish powder), mixed with enough water to form a paste
Ginger-sherry sauce
¼ cup dry sherry
2 tbsp. low-sodium soy sauce
1 tbsp. finely chopped ginger
1 tbsp. sugar
1 tbsp. honey
⅛ tsp. cayenne pepper

In a saucepan, bring 2 cups of water and the vinegar to a boil. Add the rice, tightly cover the pan and reduce the heat to medium low. Cook the rice, stirring occasionally, until all the liquid has been absorbed — about 20 minutes. Set the rice aside to cool.

While the rice is cooking, fillet the eel. Place it on its belly on a cutting board. Cut the head off behind the gills and discard it. Holding a small, sharp knife parallel to the eel, cut along one side of the dorsal fin, following the contour of the backbone along the length of the eel until the fillet is freed. Repeat the process on the other side of the fin to free the second fillet. Cut away any viscera clinging to the fillets. Rinse the fillets under cold running water and cut each in half diagonally.

Pour enough water into a large pot to fill it ½ inch deep. Put a bamboo steamer basket in the water. (Alternatively, put a heatproof cup in the center of the pot and lay a heatproof plate on top of it.) Place the eel fillets in the steamer basket or on the plate, and bring the water to a boil. Reduce the heat to low, tightly cover the pot and steam the fillets for seven minutes.

While the fillets are steaming, make the sauce. Combine the sherry, soy sauce, ginger, sugar, honey and cayenne pepper in a small saucepan. Bring the sauce to a boil, then reduce the heat to low. Simmer the sauce until it thickens and is reduced by half — seven to 10 minutes. Preheat the broiler.

Brush some of the sauce on both sides of the fillets and let them stand for five minutes. Brush more sauce on the fillets and broil them 3 inches below the heat source until they are crisp — two to four minutes. Carefully turn the fillets over, then brush on more sauce and broil them on the second side until they are crisp — two to three minutes.

While the eel is cooking, form the cooled rice into 16 ▶

cakes (the Japanese call them ''fingers''); each should be about 2 inches long, ¾ inch wide and ¾ inch thick. Arrange the rice fingers on a serving platter.

Cut the fillets diagonally into 16 pieces. Set a piece of eel atop each rice cake; brush the eel pieces with the remaining sauce and serve them with the wasabi.

EDITOR'S NOTE: *Sushi rice, a glutinous rice whose grains cohere well when cooked, has a pleasantly toothsome texture. It is available at Japanese groceries.*

Eel with Spinach and Leeks

Serves 6
Working time: about 20 minutes
Total time: about 40 minutes

Calories **370**
Protein **25g.**
Cholesterol **125mg.**
Total fat **21g.**
Saturated fat **4g.**
Sodium **130mg.**

2 lb. eel, skinned (technique, page 129), cleaned and cut into 2-inch pieces
1 tbsp. safflower oil
1 lb. leeks, trimmed, split, washed thoroughly to remove any grit, and sliced
2 garlic cloves, finely chopped
1½ tsp. fresh thyme, or ½ tsp. dried thyme leaves
2 tbsp. chopped fresh mint
1 cup dry white wine
2 cups fish stock (recipe, page 136) or unsalted chicken stock
2 lb. spinach, washed, stemmed and coarsely chopped
2 tbsp. chopped fresh parsley

Heat the oil in a large, heavy-bottomed skillet over medium heat. Add the leeks, garlic, thyme and 1 table-spoon of the mint. Sauté the mixture for two minutes. Pour in the wine, cover the skillet, and reduce the heat to medium low; cook the mixture until the leeks are tender — about 10 minutes.

Pour the stock into the pan and bring the liquid to a boil. Add the eel, reduce the heat to maintain a simmer, and cover the skillet. Cook until the eel is opaque and feels firm to the touch — about 10 minutes.

About five minutes before the eel is done, put the spinach, with only the water that clings to it from washing, in a deep pot. Set the pot over medium-high heat, cover it tightly, and steam the spinach until it is wilted — about three minutes. With a slotted spoon, transfer the spinach to a heated serving dish. Arrange the eel pieces on top of the spinach.

Add the remaining tablespoon of mint and the parsley to the eel-cooking liquid. Boil the liquid until it is reduced to 2 cups — about three minutes. Pour the sauce over the eel and serve immediately.

SUGGESTED ACCOMPANIMENT: *steamed potatoes or rice.*

Sautéed Bluefish with Toasted Hazelnuts

Serves 4
Working (and total) time: about 35 minutes

Calories **290**
Protein **26g.**
Cholesterol **75mg.**
Total fat **21g.**
Saturated fat **4g.**
Sodium **175mg.**

1 lb. bluefish fillets (or sea trout)
⅓ cup hazelnuts
2 tbsp. flour
1 tbsp. safflower oil
¼ tsp. salt
freshly ground black pepper
1 tbsp. unsalted butter
2 scallions, trimmed and thinly sliced
2 garlic cloves, finely chopped
¼ cup balsamic vinegar, or 3 tbsp. red wine vinegar mixed with 1 tsp. honey
1 tbsp. fresh lime or lemon juice
1 tomato, cored and cut into thin strips
¼ cup chopped fresh basil or Italian parsley

Preheat the oven to 350° F. Spread the hazelnuts in a single layer in a pie tin and toast them in the oven for 10 minutes. Rub the hazelnuts with a dish towel to remove most of their papery skin. Coarsely chop the nuts and set them aside.

Rinse the fillets under cold running water and pat them dry with paper towels. Cut the fillets into a total of four serving pieces and dust them with flour; pat off any excess. Heat the oil in a large, heavy-bottomed skillet over medium-high heat. Add the fillets and sauté them on one side for four minutes. Turn them over and sprinkle them with the salt and some pepper. Cook the fish on the second side until it feels firm to the touch — three to four minutes. Transfer the fillets to a serving platter and keep them warm.

Melt the butter in the skillet. Add the hazelnuts and sauté them for two minutes. Stir in the scallions, garlic, vinegar and citrus juice. Cook the mixture for one minute, stirring all the while. Add the tomato, the basil or parsley, and some pepper. Cook the mixture for one minute more, stirring constantly, then spread it evenly over the fish. Serve immediately.

SUGGESTED ACCOMPANIMENT: *baked sweet potatoes.*

Pompano on a Bed of Caramelized Shallots

Serves 4
Working (and total) time: about 30 minutes

Calories **365**
Protein **25g.**
Cholesterol **67mg.**
Total fat **18g.**
Saturated fat **7g.**
Sodium **220mg.**

2 whole pompanos (about 1½ lb. each), filleted and skinned (technique, page 130), or 1 lb. pompano fillets (or flounder or sole)
1 tbsp. safflower oil
1 lb. shallots, thinly sliced
¼ tsp. salt
1 tsp. fresh rosemary, or ¼ tsp. dried rosemary
freshly ground black pepper
¼ cup red wine vinegar
½ cup dry vermouth
½ cup fish stock (recipe, page 136)
3 tbsp. fresh lemon juice
2 garlic cloves, finely chopped
1 tbsp. light cream
1 tbsp. unsalted butter
2 rosemary sprigs for garnish

Pour the oil into a large, heavy-bottomed nonreactive skillet over medium heat. When the oil is hot, add the shallots, ⅛ teaspoon of the salt, the rosemary and some pepper. Cook, scraping the pan frequently, until the shallots are caramelized — about 25 minutes.

Add the vinegar, vermouth, stock, 2 tablespoons of the lemon juice and the garlic to the skillet. Stir the mixture until all of the caramelized juices sticking to the skillet have dissolved. Cook for three or four minutes more, then remove the skillet from the heat and stir in the cream. Transfer the mixture to a warmed serving platter and cover it with aluminum foil.

Rinse the fillets under cold running water, pat them dry with paper towels and lay them on a work surface. Wipe out the skillet and melt the butter in it over medium heat. Sprinkle the fillets with the remaining ⅛ teaspoon of salt, the remaining tablespoon of lemon juice and some pepper, and lay them in the skillet. Cook the fillets for about two minutes on the first side, then turn them and cook them on the second side until they are opaque all the way through — about two minutes more. Arrange the fillets on the warm bed of shallots. With a fork, bring a few wisps of shallot up over the edges of the fish. Garnish the fish with the rosemary sprigs and serve immediately.

SUGGESTED ACCOMPANIMENT: *steamed snow peas.*

Pompano with Kiwi Fruit

Serves 6
Working time: about 20 minutes
Total time: about 40 minutes

Calories **360**
Protein **26g.**
Cholesterol **94mg.**
Total fat **18g.**
Saturated fat **6g.**
Sodium **220mg.**

six 4½-oz. pompano fillets (or butterfish), skinned (technique, page 130)
1½ tbsp. safflower oil
2 tbsp. finely chopped shallot
½ cup dry white wine
1 lb. Jerusalem artichokes, peeled, sliced and immersed in cold water
½ cup fish stock (recipe, page 136) or water
⅜ tsp. salt
⅜ tsp. white pepper
2 kiwi fruits, peeled, one thinly sliced, the other left whole
2 tbsp. heavy cream
½ egg yolk

Heat 1 tablespoon of the oil in a saucepan over medium heat. Add the shallot and cook it, stirring frequently, until it turns translucent — three to four minutes. Pour in the wine and simmer the liquid until it is reduced by half — four to five minutes.

Drain the artichokes and add them to the saucepan along with the stock or water, ¼ teaspoon of the salt and ¼ teaspoon of the white pepper. Bring the liquid to a boil, then reduce the heat to maintain a strong simmer. Cook the artichokes until they are soft and most of the liquid has evaporated — 10 to 12 minutes. Purée the mixture together with the whole kiwi fruit in a food processor or blender for 30 seconds, stopping once to scrape down the sides. Strain the purée through a fine-meshed sieve into a bowl. In a small bowl set over ice, whip the cream until it forms soft peaks. Whisk the egg yolk into the artichoke purée, then gently stir in the whipped cream.

Rinse the fillets under cold running water and pat ▶

them dry with paper towels. Place the fillets in a shallow flameproof casserole and sprinkle the remaining ⅛ teaspoon of salt and the remaining ⅛ teaspoon of pepper over them. Brush the tops of the fillets with the remaining ½ tablespoon of oil. Broil the fillets about 3½ inches below the heat source for two minutes. Turn the fillets over and broil them for an additional two minutes; they should be barely cooked.

Spoon the artichoke purée over the fillets. Broil the fish just below the heat source, turning the dish once or twice to ensure even browning, until the purée is lightly browned — one to two minutes. Arrange the kiwi fruit slices on top of the purée. Serve the glazed fillets immediately.

SUGGESTED ACCOMPANIMENT: *sautéed cherry tomatoes.*

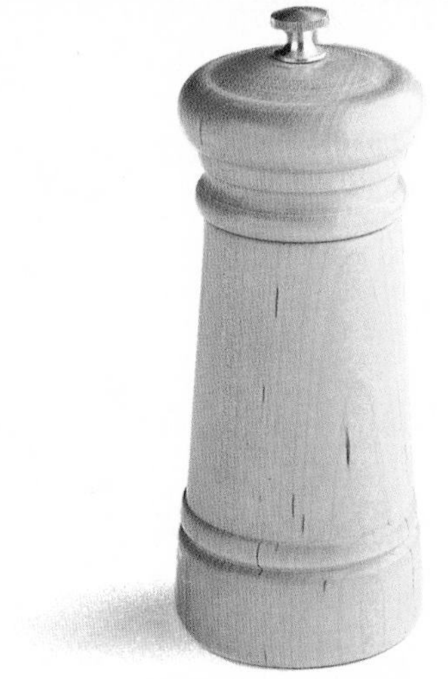

Salmon with Fresh Basil Sauce

Serves 4
Working time: about 15 minutes
Total time: about 30 minutes

Calories **285**
Protein **24g.**
Cholesterol **61mg.**
Total fat **18g.**
Saturated fat **6g.**
Sodium **190mg.**

1 lb. red or silver salmon fillets, skinned (technique, page 130)
1 tbsp. safflower oil
¼ tsp. salt
freshly ground black pepper
1½ tbsp. fresh lemon juice
2 shallots, thinly sliced
1 garlic clove, finely chopped
2 cups loosely packed basil leaves
¼ cup fish stock (recipe, page 136) or dry white wine
¼ cup heavy cream

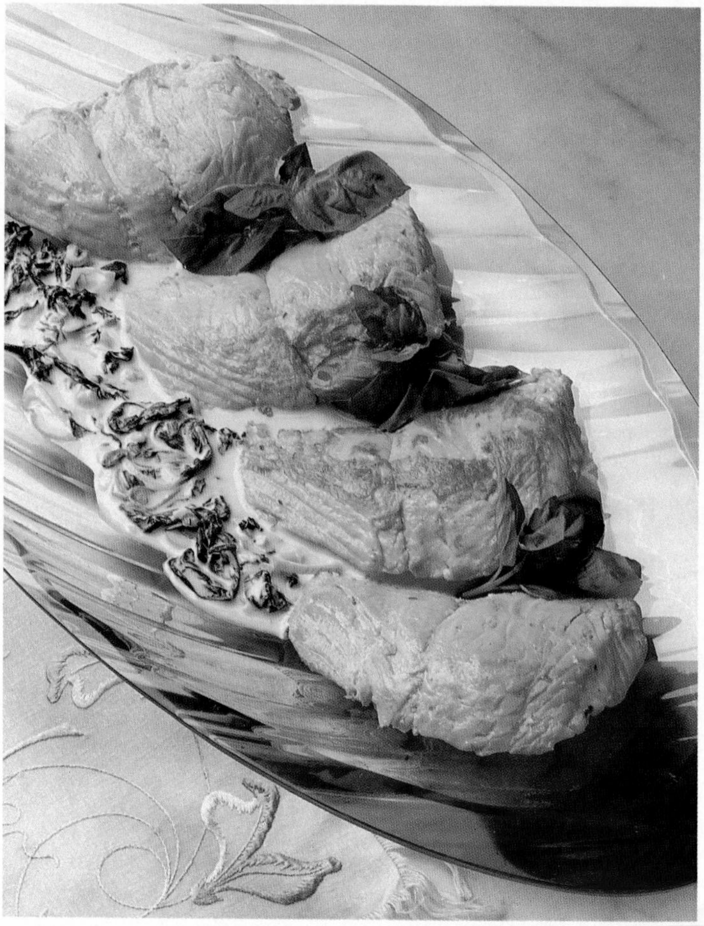

Rinse the fillets under cold running water and pat them dry with paper towels. Cut the fish diagonally across the grain into slices about 1 inch thick.

Pour the oil into a large, heavy-bottomed skillet over high heat. When the oil is hot, add the fish pieces and cook them on the first side for three minutes. Carefully turn the pieces over and sprinkle them with ⅛ teaspoon of the salt, a generous grinding of pepper and the lemon juice. Cook them on the second side until they are barely done — about three minutes more. Remove the pan from the heat.

Transfer the fish to a warmed serving platter and cover the platter with aluminum foil. Return the skillet to the stove over medium heat. Add the shallots and garlic and cook them, stirring constantly, for 30 seconds. Add the basil and the stock or wine, and simmer the mixture for one minute. Stir in the cream, the remaining ⅛ teaspoon of salt and some more pepper, and continue simmering the sauce until it thickens slightly — about two minutes. Pour the sauce over the fish and serve immediately.

SUGGESTED ACCOMPANIMENT: *grilled red peppers.*

Pickled Salmon and Red Potatoes

Serves 6 as a first course
Working time: about 25 minutes
Total time: 24 hours

Calories **250**
Protein **24g.**
Cholesterol **40mg.**
Total fat **11g.**
Saturated fat **2g.**
Sodium **115mg.**

1½ lb. red or silver salmon fillets, skinned (technique, page 130)
1 cup lightly packed fresh dill sprigs
2 tbsp. virgin olive oil
1¼ cups red wine vinegar or white wine vinegar
juice of 1 lemon
juice of 1 orange
1 bunch scallions, trimmed and sliced diagonally into ½-inch pieces
1 tbsp. mustard seeds
1 tsp. black peppercorns, cracked
3 bay leaves
½ tsp. salt
1 tsp. whole cloves
1 lb. red potatoes, the skin left on

Rinse the fillets under cold running water and pat them dry with paper towels. Cut the fish into chunks about ¾ inch thick.

In a large glass bowl, combine the salmon chunks, ¾ cup of the dill sprigs and the oil. Put the vinegar, lemon juice, orange juice, scallions, mustard seeds, pepper, bay leaves, salt and cloves in a large, nonreactive saucepan. Bring the mixture to a boil, then pour it over the salmon chunks. Gently stir the marinade and salmon to coat the pieces. Allow the marinade to cool, then cover the bowl and refrigerate it for at least 24 hours.

At the end of the marinating time, strain ¾ cup of the marinade into a second glass bowl. Add the remaining ¼ cup of dill sprigs to the strained marinade. Cut the potatoes into 1-inch pieces and place them in a steamer. Fill a saucepan about 1 inch deep with water. Put the steamer in the saucepan, cover the pan and bring the water to a simmer. Steam the potatoes until they are soft — 10 to 15 minutes. Immediately transfer the potatoes to the strained marinade; stir gently to coat the potatoes.

Serve the hot potatoes at once with the cold salmon.

SUGGESTED ACCOMPANIMENT: *pumpernickel bread.*

Whole Poached Salmon

Serves 8
Working (and total) time: about 30 minutes

Calories **280**	one 4-lb. whole salmon, gutted (technique, pages 128-129)
Protein **28g.**	4 quarts court bouillon (recipe, page 136)
Cholesterol **111mg.**	**Garnish**
Total fat **17g.**	¼ lb. spinach, washed, stemmed and sliced thinly
Saturated fat **4g.**	½ lb. daikon radish, peeled and julienned
Sodium **90mg.**	1 red plum, pitted and sliced

Pour the court bouillon into a fish poacher or pan large enough to accommodate the salmon.

Wash the salmon inside and out under cold running water. Wrap the salmon in a double thickness of cheesecloth that is about 10 inches longer than the fish. Knot each end of the cheesecloth and secure it by tying string around the fish in two or three places.

Holding the knotted ends of the cloth, gently lower the fish into the court bouillon. Bring the liquid to a simmer over medium heat. Cover the pan, reduce the heat to low, and cook the salmon for eight minutes per inch of thickness (measured at its thickest point).

Let the fish cool in the court bouillon, then carefully transfer it to a work surface. Cut away the strings, untie the knots, and unwrap the cheesecloth, leaving the fish on the cloth. Cut out all but the pectoral fins of the fish. Make a long cut down the back and down the belly of the salmon. Cut through the skin at the base of the tail. Then, working from the base of the tail toward the head, gently pull off the skin in strips. Discard the skin.

Carefully transfer the fish to a long platter, placing it skinned side down. Make another cut at the base of the tail and remove the skin from the second side.

Combine the sliced spinach and julienned radish and arrange them around the salmon. Garnish with the plum slices. Serve the salmon warm or cold, accompanied by any number of the sauces that follow.

Each of the sauce recipes below yields one third of the amount of sauce necessary to accompany the salmon. If you decide to make only one, remember to triple the ingredients.

Spinach-and-Garlic Sauce

Makes about 1 cup
Working (and total) time: about 15 minutes

Calories **20**	1 lb. spinach, washed and stemmed
Protein **1g.**	1 tbsp. safflower oil
Cholesterol **0mg.**	2 garlic cloves, finely chopped
Total fat **2g.**	⅔ cup fish stock (recipe, page 136)
Saturated fat **0g.**	¼ tsp. salt
Sodium **85mg.**	⅛ tsp. white pepper
	pinch of nutmeg

Place the spinach, with just the water that clings to its leaves, in a large saucepan over high heat. Cover the pan and steam the spinach until it is wilted — one to

two minutes. Drain it well. Squeeze the spinach with your hands to rid it of excess liquid, then chop the spinach coarsely and set it aside.

Heat the oil in a small saucepan over medium heat. Add the garlic and cook it for about 30 seconds. Add the spinach, stock, salt, pepper and nutmeg, and simmer the mixture for three minutes. Transfer the mixture to a food processor or blender and purée it. Pour the sauce into a serving bowl. Serve the sauce warm with the poached salmon.

Radish-and-Ginger Sauce

Makes about 1 cup
Working time: about 15 minutes
Total time: about 25 minutes

Calories **40**	1 tbsp. safflower oil
Protein **1g.**	1 small onion, finely chopped
Cholesterol **3mg.**	2 tbsp. finely chopped fresh ginger
Total fat **3g.**	½ lb. daikon radish, peeled and thinly sliced
Saturated fat **1g.**	½ cup fish stock (recipe, page 136)
Sodium **80mg.**	¼ tsp. salt
	⅛ tsp. white pepper
	¼ cup sour cream
	¼ cup plain low-fat yogurt

Heat the oil in a small saucepan over medium heat. Add the onion and cook it, stirring occasionally, until it is transparent — three to four minutes. Stir in the ginger and cook for one minute more. Add the daikon radish and the stock; simmer the mixture, partially covered, until the radish is tender — about 10 minutes.

Transfer the mixture to a food processor or blender and purée it. Add an additional tablespoon of stock or water, if necessary, to achieve a smooth consistency. Transfer the purée to a bowl and stir in the salt and pepper, then fold in the sour cream and the yogurt. Spoon the sauce into a serving bowl and serve it with the poached salmon.

Plum Sauce with Chutney

Makes about 1 cup
Working (and total) time: about 15 minutes

Calories **50**	¾ lb. red plums, halved and pitted
Protein **0g.**	¼ cup mango chutney
Cholesterol **0mg.**	¼ cup dry white wine
Total fat **0g.**	
Saturated fat **0g.**	
Sodium **20mg.**	

Combine the plums, chutney and wine in a small saucepan over medium-low heat, and bring the liquid to a simmer. Cover the pan and cook the mixture until the plums have softened — about seven minutes. Transfer the mixture to a food processor or blender and purée it. Pour the sauce into a serving bowl. Serve the sauce with the poached salmon.

Broiled Trout and Dried Figs

Serves 4
Working time: about 1 hour
Total time: about 1 hour and 10 minutes

Calories **435**
Protein **33g.**
Cholesterol **94mg.**
Total fat **11g.**
Saturated fat **2g.**
Sodium **255mg.**

4 trout (about ¾ lb. each), gutted, the fins removed
12 dried figs, halved lengthwise
1 cup medium-dry sherry
3 tbsp. balsamic vinegar or sherry vinegar
1 tbsp. maple syrup or honey
1 tbsp. Dijon mustard
¼ tsp. salt
freshly ground black pepper

Put the figs in a nonreactive saucepan over low heat with the sherry and 2 tablespoons of the vinegar. Simmer the figs for 10 minutes. Remove the pan from the heat and let the figs steep in the liquid.

While the figs are steeping, butterfly the trout: Cut off and discard the heads of the trout. With a small, sharp knife, cut through the back of a trout on one side of its backbone from the head to within 1 inch of the tail. Repeat the cutting procedure on the other side of the backbone. Using kitchen scissors, sever the backbone near the tail; lift it out with your fingers. With tweezers, pull out any small bones remaining in the trout. Rinse the fish under cold running water, then pat it dry with paper towels. Repeat these steps to butterfly the remaining trout.

Preheat the broiler. Remove the figs from their steeping liquid and set them aside. Stir the maple syrup or honey into the liquid, then cook the liquid over medium heat until only about ⅓ cup remains — approximately five minutes. Whisk the mustard and the remaining tablespoon of vinegar into the sauce. Remove the pan from the heat.

Set the butterflied trout, skin side down, on a broiler pan and tuck their sides under slightly. Sprinkle the fish with the salt and pepper and brush them with about half of the sauce. Broil the trout 3 inches below the heat source until their flesh is opaque — about five minutes. Put the figs on the broiler pan with the fish. Brush the fish and figs with the remaining sauce and broil them together for one minute before serving.

SUGGESTED ACCOMPANIMENT: *stir-fried carrots.*

Baked Lake Trout Stuffed with Kumquats and Collard Greens

Serves 8
Working time: about 45 minutes
Total time: about 1 hour and 15 minutes

Calories **290**
Protein **24g.**
Cholesterol **52mg.**
Total fat **18g.**
Saturated fat **4g.**
Sodium **280mg.**

one 5-lb. lake trout, scaled and filleted, skin left on (techniques, pages 128, 130)
2 garlic cloves, finely chopped
2 tbsp. fresh lemon juice
¾ tsp. salt
freshly ground black pepper
2 tbsp. unsalted butter
2 tbsp. safflower oil
2 medium leeks, trimmed, split, washed thoroughly to remove any grit, and thinly sliced
1½ tsp. fresh thyme, or ½ tsp. dried thyme leaves
¼ lb. fresh kumquats, thinly sliced and seeded
¾ lb. collard greens, washed, stemmed and chopped
½ cup dry bread crumbs

Run your fingers over the fillets to locate any small bones; using tweezers, carefully pull out the bones. Rinse the fillets under cold running water and pat them dry with paper towels. Rub the fillets with the garlic, lemon juice, ½ teaspoon of the salt and some pepper. Set the fillets aside while you prepare the stuffing.

Preheat the oven to 375° F. Put the butter and 1 tablespoon of the oil in a large, heavy-bottomed skillet over medium heat. When the butter has melted, add the leeks and thyme; cook, stirring occasionally, for five minutes. Stir in the kumquats and cook for two minutes more. Add the collard greens, the remaining ¼ teaspoon of salt and some more pepper. Cook the mixture until the collard greens are wilted and tender — five to seven minutes. Stir in the bread crumbs and remove the pan from the heat.

Lay one of the trout fillets skin side down in a large, lightly oiled baking dish. Spread the collard-kumquat mixture over the fillet. Lay the remaining fillet skin side up on the stuffing. Brush the remaining tablespoon of oil over the top of the fish.

Bake the assembly until the fillets are opaque and the filling is hot — 25 to 30 minutes. Carefully transfer the fish to a serving platter, slice, and serve.

SUGGESTED ACCOMPANIMENT: *baked potatoes with chives.*

Soufflé of Smoked Trout

Serves 6
Working time: about 30 minutes
Total time: about 1 hour and 20 minutes

Calories **225**
Protein **24g.**
Cholesterol **146mg.**
Total fat **9g.**
Saturated fat **3g.**
Sodium **305mg.**

1 small smoked trout fillet, skinned and boned, the flesh shredded (about 2 oz.)
4 fresh-water trout, filleted (about 1 lb. of fillets; technique, page 130) or 1 lb. sea trout fillets
2 tbsp. finely cut fresh dill
2 tbsp. fresh lemon juice
1 tbsp. unsalted butter
1 onion, finely chopped
6 tbsp. flour
1 cup skim milk
1 cup fish stock (recipe, page 136), or an additional cup of skim milk
¼ tsp. fresh thyme, or ⅛ tsp. dried thyme leaves
⅛ tsp. grated nutmeg
¼ tsp. salt
freshly ground black pepper
2 egg yolks
8 egg whites
⅛ tsp. cream of tartar

Preheat the oven to 425° F. Rinse the fresh trout fillets under cold running water and pat them dry with paper towels. Wrap the fillets in a single piece of aluminum foil, its dull side out, and set the foil package on a baking sheet. Bake the fillets until they are opaque — approximately 15 minutes.

Unwrap the fillets and spread them out to cool. Flake the flesh with a fork, carefully picking out all the bones. In a large bowl, combine the fresh trout with the smoked trout, the dill and the lemon juice. Set the fish mixture aside.

Melt the butter in a heavy-bottomed saucepan over medium-high heat. Add the onion and cook it until it is translucent — about four minutes. While the onion is cooking, put the flour in a bowl and stir in the milk and the stock, if you are using it. Pour this mixture into the saucepan and bring it to a boil, whisking constantly. Remove the pan from the heat and whisk in the thyme, nutmeg, salt, pepper and egg yolks; set the mixture aside and keep it warm.

Put the egg whites in a bowl with the cream of tartar; with a whisk or an electric mixer, beat the egg whites into stiff peaks. Stir the milk-and-stock mixture

into the fish mixture. Stir about one fourth of the egg whites into the fish mixture, then gently fold in the remaining whites.

Pour the mixture into a lightly buttered 2-quart soufflé dish; the mixture should come to within ½ inch of the rim. Put the dish in the oven. Immediately reduce the oven temperature to 375° F. Bake the soufflé until it is puffed and golden and the center has set — about 45 minutes. Serve immediately.

SUGGESTED ACCOMPANIMENT: *Belgian endive and radicchio salad.*

Cucumber-Stuffed Butterfish with Dill Sauce

Serves 4
Working time: about 30 minutes
Total time: about 40 minutes

Calories **440**
Protein **29g.**
Cholesterol **79mg.**
Total fat **23g.**
Saturated fat **4g.**
Sodium **430mg.**

4 whole butterfish, about ½ lb. each (or ocean perch or porgy), cleaned, scaled and filleted (technique, page 130), the skin left on
2½ tbsp. safflower oil
1 cucumber, peeled and thinly sliced
1 tbsp. finely chopped shallot
¼ tsp. salt
freshly ground black pepper
¼ cup dry vermouth
½ cup flour
2 egg whites, lightly beaten
1 cup dry bread crumbs
dill sprigs for garnish
Dill sauce
1 cup finely cut fresh dill
1 cup plain low-fat yogurt
1 tbsp. dried dillweed
2 tbsp. finely chopped shallot
⅛ tsp. salt
⅛ tsp. white pepper

Preheat the oven to 375° F.

Pour ½ tablespoon of the oil into a large, ovenproof skillet over medium-high heat. Add the cucumber and sauté it until it begins to soften — about two minutes. Add the shallot and cook it, stirring constantly, until it turns translucent — one to two minutes. Reduce the heat to low; season the vegetables with ⅛ teaspoon of the salt and some black pepper. Pour in the vermouth and simmer the mixture until nearly all the liquid has evaporated — about three minutes. Remove the skillet from the heat and set it aside.

To prepare the dill sauce, fold the cut fresh dill into the yogurt along with the dried dillweed, shallot, salt

and white pepper.

Lay one half of each filleted fish skin side down on a work surface. Season the fish with some black pepper and the remaining ⅛ teaspoon of salt. Arrange a layer of cucumber slices on each half, reserving four slices for garnish. Lay the remaining fillets atop their respective halves to form fish packets.

Holding a fish packet together like a sandwich, press each side first into the flour, then into the egg white, and last into the bread crumbs. Wipe out the skillet, set it over medium heat and pour in the remaining 2 tablespoons of oil. Fry the fish packets on one side until they are lightly browned — about two minutes. Turn them over and transfer the skillet to the oven; bake the fish until they can be easily flaked with a fork at the thickest point — four to five minutes.

Carefully transfer the fish to a warm platter. Spoon some of the dill sauce over each fish packet. Garnish the packets with the reserved cucumber slices and the dill sprigs; serve the remaining sauce on the side.

EDITOR'S NOTE: *Although some small butterfish appear to have no scales at all, numerous small scales are clustered around the head; these need to be removed.*
The dried dillweed in this recipe is used to intensify the flavor of the fresh dill.

Mackerel Brochettes

Serves 4
Working time: about 45 minutes
Total time: about 1 hour and 45 minutes

Calories **485**
Protein **31g.**
Cholesterol **135mg.**
Total fat **20g.**
Saturated fat **4g.**
Sodium **220mg.**

1 lb. mackerel fillets (or salmon or tuna steaks)
1 head of fennel, the base cut into ½-inch squares, the feathery tops reserved
8 pearl onions, unpeeled
1 garlic clove
⅛ tsp. salt
juice of 1 lemon
½ cup dry white wine
1 tsp. fresh thyme, or ½ tsp. dried thyme leaves
8 cherry tomatoes
1 medium zucchini, sliced into ¾-inch-thick slices
8 button mushrooms, wiped clean
½ lb. fresh spinach fettuccine
Peppery tomato sauce
1 tbsp. virgin olive oil
2 shallots, finely chopped
2 garlic cloves, finely chopped
2½ lb. ripe tomatoes, peeled, seeded and coarsely chopped
1 tsp. fresh thyme, or ½ tsp. dried thyme leaves
⅛ tsp. salt
⅛ tsp. cayenne pepper
freshly ground black pepper

Rinse the fillets under cold running water and pat them dry with paper towels. Cut the fish into chunks about 1 inch thick.

Cook the fennel squares in boiling water for three

minutes. Remove the fennel with a slotted spoon. Parboil the pearl onions for three minutes; when they are cool enough to handle, peel them.

To prepare the marinade, pound together the garlic and salt into a paste in a large bowl. Stir in the lemon juice, wine and thyme. Finely chop enough of the feathery fennel tops to yield 1 tablespoon. Add the chopped fennel tops to the marinade; reserve the remaining tops for garnish. Add the fish, fennel squares, pearl onions, cherry tomatoes, zucchini and mushrooms to the bowl. Stir gently to coat the fish and vegetables with the marinade. Refrigerate the mixture for one hour, stirring it from time to time.

To make the sauce, heat the oil in a large, heavy-bottomed skillet over low heat. Add the shallots and garlic, and cook them, stirring occasionally, until the shallots are soft — about five minutes. Stir in the tomatoes, then the thyme, salt, cayenne pepper and some black pepper. Cook the sauce for 15 minutes, then, using a wooden spoon, push the sauce through a sieve into a small saucepan and keep it warm.

Preheat the grill or broiler. Put 3 quarts of water on to boil with 1½ teaspoons of salt. Thread the fish and vegetables onto eight long skewers. Cook the brochettes, turning occasionally, until the fish is browned and the vegetables are tender — eight to 10 minutes.

While the brochettes are cooking, add the fettuccine to the boiling water. Start testing the fettuccine after two minutes and cook it until it is *al dente*. Drain the pasta and toss it with the tomato sauce.

Divide the pasta evenly among four plates; place two brochettes on each plate. Garnish the servings with the reserved fennel tops and serve immediately.

Mackerel Fillets with Rhubarb Sauce

Serves 4
Working time: about 10 minutes
Total time: about 40 minutes

Calories **325**	
Protein **22g.**	1 lb. mackerel fillets (or sea trout), the skin left on
Cholesterol **91mg.**	2 tbsp. sugar
Total fat **16g.**	1 tbsp. red wine vinegar
Saturated fat **3g.**	2 navel oranges, the julienned zest and juice of one reserved, the other peeled and sliced into thin rounds
Sodium **175mg.**	½ lb. rhubarb, thinly sliced
	⅛ tsp. ground cumin
	¼ tsp. salt
	freshly ground black pepper
	1 tbsp. safflower oil

In a small, heavy-bottomed nonreactive saucepan over high heat, cook the sugar, stirring constantly with a wooden spoon, until it melts and forms a syrup. Cook the syrup, stirring all the while, until it turns a light caramel color — 30 seconds to one minute. (If the sugar turns dark brown, discard it and start over.) Standing well back to avoid being splattered, immediately pour in the vinegar and orange juice; the sugar will harden. Reduce the heat to medium low and cook the mixture until it becomes syrupy again — three to five minutes.

Add the orange zest, rhubarb, cumin and ⅛ teaspoon of the salt to the saucepan. Cover the pan and cook the mixture until the rhubarb is soft and has begun to lose its shape — about 15 minutes. Purée the mixture in a food mill or blender. If you are using a blender, strain the rhubarb after it has been puréed.

While the rhubarb is cooking, preheat the broiler. Rinse the fillets under cold running water and pat them dry with paper towels. Sprinkle the remaining ⅛ teaspoon of salt and some pepper over the skinless side of the fillets. Place the fish skin side down on a baking sheet and brush the tops with the oil. Broil the fillets about 3½ inches below the heat source for six minutes, then turn the fillets skin side up and cook them for two minutes more. To test for doneness, insert a fork into a fillet at its thickest point; the flesh should be opaque all the way through.

Gently transfer the fillets to a serving platter and spoon the rhubarb sauce over them; arrange the orange slices on top as a garnish.

SUGGESTED ACCOMPANIMENT: *sautéed mushrooms.*

3 *A harvest of scallops, clams, lobsters, crayfish, Dungeness and blue crabs, stone-crab claws, oysters and mussels suggests the abundance of American waters.*

Shellfish's Manifold Pleasures

Shellfish, which abound along the margins of the oceans in an almost unbelievable variety, are savored the world over. They can be conveniently grouped into three basic categories. The common bivalve mollusks include the clam, oyster and mussel. Among the crustaceans are shrimp, lobster, crab and crayfish. Octopus and squid, though mollusks, have no outer shells and belong to a group called the cephalopods.

While most mollusks and crustaceans have slightly less protein than finned fish, they are well endowed with minerals. Like tiny biological factories, they concentrate vital trace elements from sea water — iron, copper, iodine and zinc, among others. Recent findings suggest that the presence of plant sterols in clams, oysters and mussels helps to reduce bodily absorption of the cholesterol they do contain. Squid, octopus and shrimp, on the other hand, contain relatively high levels of cholesterol. Blue crabs, although lower in cholesterol than the others, still have about one third the amount allowable for a day's eating.

The one essential in shellfish cookery is absolute freshness. The freshest clams, mussels and oysters are sold live in their shells — which means that they must be cleaned and shucked at home (technique, page 135). To reduce the risk of eating contaminated shellfish, be sure to buy them from a reliable fishmonger.

Shellfish can be served in limitless ways. Oysters and clams may be eaten raw, or like mussels, they may be steamed in their shells, with results that are both healthful and mouth watering. Scallops almost always come to American markets minus their shells. They lend themselves readily to steaming, sautéing, broiling and baking. But as with all bivalves, care must be taken to avoid overcooking them. A scallop — or a clam or oyster, for that matter — cooked for more than a minute or two will turn rubbery.

The shell-less mollusks — octopus and squid — each require different cooking strategies. A small piece of cartilage, known as a pen or quill, runs through the squid's body, and this must be removed, along with the ink sac, before cooking (techniques, page 132). The flesh of squid and octopus is tender, especially that of smaller specimens. It can be stir fried quickly, but it toughens after a few minutes over heat; then, if cooked longer, as in the squid stew with red wine on page 109, it will soften again. Squid can be slashed with a knife to make its meat more supple. Many cooks recommend pounding larger squid and octopus with a mallet to tenderize them before cooking.

Steaming and poaching are the classic techniques for handling crustaceans. They may also be broiled or grilled, or their meat can be stir fried with vegetables. The 40 recipes that follow explore all these methods.

Steamed, Spiced Crabs

Serves 4
Working time: about 20 minutes
Total time: about 45 minutes

Calories **115**
Protein **17g.**
Cholesterol **78mg.**
Total fat **1g.**
Saturated fat **0g.**
Sodium **135mg.**

12 live blue crabs
¼ cup finely chopped fresh ginger
1 whole garlic bulb, the cloves peeled and finely chopped
1 tbsp. mustard seeds
½ tsp. ground allspice
2 tsp. hot red-pepper flakes, crushed
6 bay leaves, crushed
1 tbsp. fennel seeds
2 onions, finely chopped
1 cup cider vinegar
1 cup dry white wine

If the crabs are sandy, wash each one under cold running water, holding it with kitchen tongs.

Combine the ginger, garlic, mustard seeds, allspice, red pepper, bay leaves, fennel seeds and onions in a bowl. Set a steamer in a tall stockpot and pour in the vinegar, wine and 2 cups of water. Bring the liquid to a boil, then remove the pot from the heat.

Put three crabs in the steamer and scatter a quarter of the spice-and-onion mixture over them. Layer the remaining crabs on top, with three crabs and a quarter of the spice mixture in each layer. Cover the pot tightly and set it over high heat.

Steam the crabs for 20 minutes, timing from the moment when steam first escapes from the pot. At the end of the steaming period, turn off the heat and let the pot stand, still covered, while the steam subsides — about three minutes.

Serve the crabs hot, providing a mallet for cracking the claws, nutpicks for extracting the meat, and plenty of napkins.

SUGGESTED ACCOMPANIMENTS: *corn on the cob; potato salad.*

Batter-Dipped Soft-Shell Crabs with Ham and Scallions

Serves 6
Working time: about 50 minutes
Total time: about 1 hour

Calories **285**
Protein **35g.**
Cholesterol **154mg.**
Total fat **8g.**
Saturated fat **1g.**
Sodium **560mg.**

12 soft-shell crabs, cleaned and trimmed
¾ cup light beer
¾ cup flour
3 tbsp. grainy mustard
2 tbsp. safflower oil
freshly ground black pepper
1 oz. lean ham, diced
2 scallions, trimmed and thinly sliced
1 lemon, cut into 6 wedges

Preheat the oven to 375° F. Lightly oil a baking sheet large enough to hold the crabs in one layer, and set the baking sheet aside.

Pour the beer into a large bowl. Gradually whisk the flour into the beer until a smooth batter results. Stir in the mustard and set the batter aside.

Heat 1 tablespoon of the oil in a large nonstick or heavy-bottomed skillet over medium-high heat. Sprinkle the crabs with some pepper. Dip six of the crabs in the batter, lightly shaking off any excess, and place them in the skillet. Cook the crabs on the first side until they are browned — about 45 seconds — then carefully turn them over and brown them on the second side for 45 seconds. Transfer the crabs to the baking sheet.

Wipe the skillet clean and return it to the heat. Pour in the remaining tablespoon of oil. Dip the remaining six crabs in the batter and brown them in the skillet the same way you cooked the first batch. Transfer the second batch to the baking sheet.

Bake the crabs for eight minutes. Remove the crabs from the oven and scatter the ham and scallions over them, then return them to the oven and bake for two minutes more. Serve the crabs immediately, with the lemon wedges alongside.

SUGGESTED ACCOMPANIMENT: *green bean salad.*

Asian Crab-and-Vegetable Salad

Serves 6 as a luncheon salad
Working time: about 35 minutes
Total time: about 1 hour

Calories **165**
Protein **15g.**
Cholesterol **57mg.**
Total fat **6g.**
Saturated fat **1g.**
Sodium **250mg.**

1 lb. cooked crab meat, picked over
juice of 1 lemon
¼ tsp. salt
freshly ground black pepper
1 tsp. dry mustard
2 tbsp. chopped fresh ginger
2 tsp. rice vinegar
1 garlic clove, finely chopped
2 tbsp. dry white wine
2 tbsp. peanut oil
¼ tsp. dark sesame oil
1 small cucumber, peeled, seeded and sliced, the slices quartered
1 cup sliced fresh bamboo shoots, blanched for 1 minute and drained, or 1 cup canned sliced bamboo shoots, blanched for 10 seconds and drained
1 cup peeled and sliced fresh water chestnuts, blanched for 1 minute and drained, or 1 cup canned sliced water chestnuts, drained
¼ lb. snow peas, strings removed, julienned
2 tbsp. chopped pimiento
2 heads Boston lettuce, the leaves washed and patted dry

In a large bowl, combine the crab meat with the lemon juice, ⅛ teaspoon of the salt and some pepper. Refrigerate the mixture while you assemble the remaining ingredients for the salad.

To make the dressing, first put the mustard in a bowl. Place the ginger in a piece of cheesecloth and squeeze it over the bowl to extract the juice; discard the ginger. Pour in the vinegar and whisk well, then add the garlic and wine, and whisk again. Let the mixture stand for five minutes before whisking in the peanut oil and sesame oil. Add the remaining ⅛ teaspoon of salt and some more pepper. Set the dressing aside.

Add the cucumber, bamboo shoots, water chestnuts, snow peas and pimiento to the crab meat, and mix well. Pour the dressing over the salad and toss gently. Chill the salad for 30 minutes.

To serve, arrange the lettuce leaves on individual serving plates. Spoon the salad into the leaves and serve immediately.

Crab-Potato Patties

Serves 6 (makes 12 patties)
Working time: about 30 minutes
Total time: about 1 hour

Calories **215**
Protein **17g.**
Cholesterol **63mg.**
Total fat **8g.**
Saturated fat **2g.**
Sodium **300mg.**

1 lb. crab meat, picked over
1 lb. potatoes, boiled, cooled, peeled and coarsely grated
¾ cup finely chopped onion
½ cup finely chopped fresh parsley
3 tbsp. finely cut dill
1 tbsp. dry sherry
2 tbsp. plain low-fat yogurt
2 egg whites, beaten
¼ tsp. salt
¼ tsp. freshly ground black pepper
¼ tsp. ground mace
⅛ tsp. cayenne pepper
¾ cup dry bread crumbs
1 tbsp. unsalted butter
2 tbsp. safflower oil
parsley sprigs for garnish
2 lemons, cut into wedges

Preheat the broiler. In a large mixing bowl, combine the crab meat, potatoes, onion, chopped parsley, dill, sherry, yogurt, egg whites, salt, pepper, mace and cayenne pepper; mix gently until the ingredients are thoroughly combined.

Form the mixture into 12 patties, each about ½ inch thick. Dredge each patty in the bread crumbs to coat it completely. Put the patties on a lightly-buttered broiler pan as you work. Melt the butter and oil together; drizzle half of this mixture over the tops of the patties.

Broil the patties until they turn a crusty golden brown — three to five minutes. Turn the patties over and drizzle the remaining butter mixture over them. Broil the patties for three to five minutes more. Serve immediately, garnished with the parsley sprigs and the lemon wedges.

SUGGESTED ACCOMPANIMENT: *steamed julienned carrots and zucchini with fresh herbs.*

Crab-Stuffed Mushroom Caps

Serves 12 as an hors d'oeuvre
Working time: about 25 minutes
Total time: about 50 minutes

Calories **100**
Protein **8g.**
Cholesterol **21mg.**
Total fat **4g.**
Saturated fat **2g.**
Sodium **135mg.**

½ lb. crab meat, picked over
1½ cups fish stock (recipe, page 136)
juice of 1 lemon
36 large mushrooms (about 2½ lb.), wiped clean, the stems carefully removed and finely chopped
2 tbsp. finely chopped shallot
½ cup dry vermouth
2 tsp. fresh thyme, or ½ tsp. dried thyme leaves
1 tbsp. unsalted butter
2 tbsp. flour
¾ cup low-fat milk
⅛ tsp. salt
grated nutmeg
white pepper
½ cup freshly grated Parmesan cheese
¼ cup coarsely chopped fresh basil
2 tbsp. unsalted pistachio nuts, crushed

In a large, nonreactive skillet, heat 1 cup of the stock and the lemon juice over medium heat. Add the mushroom caps and toss them gently to coat them with the liquid. Cover the skillet and poach the mushrooms, turning them occasionally to ensure even cooking, until they are cooked through — six to seven minutes.

With a slotted spoon, transfer the mushrooms to a platter lined with paper towels. Add the shallot to the skillet along with the chopped mushroom stems, the vermouth and the thyme. Bring the liquid to a boil, then reduce the heat to medium and cook the mixture at a brisk simmer, stirring occasionally, until all but 2 tablespoons of the liquid has evaporated — about 15 minutes. Set the mushroom mixture aside.

Melt the butter in a small saucepan over medium heat. Whisk in the flour to form a paste, and cook the paste for three minutes. Stirring constantly to prevent lumps from forming, slowly pour in the milk, then the remaining ½ cup of stock. Add the salt and sprinkle in some nutmeg and white pepper. Simmer the sauce until it thickens — about three minutes. Stir in the cheese and the basil.

Preheat the broiler. To complete the filling, combine the crab meat with the mushroom mixture in a bowl. Slowly pour the sauce into the bowl and stir gently to coat the stuffing. Mound ¾ tablespoon of stuffing in the hollow of each mushroom cap. Broil the stuffed mushrooms 3 inches below the heat source until the crab begins to brown — about three minutes. Sprinkle the pistachios over the top of the mushrooms and serve them hot.

Scallops in Fermented Black-Bean Sauce

Serves 4
Working (and total) time: 15 minutes

Calories **185**
Protein **20g.**
Cholesterol **41mg.**
Total fat **7g.**
Saturated fat **1g.**
Sodium **235mg.**

1 lb. bay scallops
2 tbsp. apricot preserves or orange marmalade
¼ cup fresh lime juice
1½ tbsp. fermented black beans, rinsed
1 tbsp. chopped fresh ginger
freshly ground black pepper
1½ tbsp. safflower oil

To prepare the sauce, combine the preserves or marmalade, lime juice, black beans, ginger and some pepper in a small bowl. Set the sauce aside.

Rinse the scallops under cold running water. Heat the oil in a large, heavy-bottomed skillet over high heat. When the oil is hot, add the scallops and cook them, stirring constantly, for one minute. Add the sauce and continue cooking, stirring all the while, for one minute more. With a slotted spoon, transfer the scallops to a heated platter. Cook the sauce, stirring, until it is reduced by half — one to two minutes. Pour the sauce over the scallops and serve immediately.

SUGGESTED ACCOMPANIMENT: *green beans.*

Chilled Scallops and Asparagus

Serves 4
Working time: about 45 minutes
Total time: about 1 hour

Calories **205**
Protein **15g.**
Cholesterol **31mg.**
Total fat **11g.**
Saturated fat **1g.**
Sodium **210mg.**

¾ lb. sea scallops, the bright white connective tissue removed, or ¾ lb. bay scallops
1 tbsp. safflower oil
1½ tsp. fresh lime juice
¼ tsp. salt
¾ lb. asparagus, trimmed and julienned
1 navel orange, peeled and cut into sections
Scallion-orange vinaigrette
3 scallions, trimmed and finely chopped
juice of 1 navel orange
1½ tbsp. red wine vinegar
½ tsp. sugar
1 tsp. fresh thyme, or ¼ tsp. dried thyme leaves
1 tbsp. julienned orange zest
1 tbsp. virgin olive oil
1 tbsp. safflower oil

To make the vinaigrette, combine the scallions with the orange juice, vinegar, sugar, thyme and orange zest in a small bowl. Let the mixture stand for at least 10 minutes, then whisk in the olive oil and safflower oil. Set the vinaigrette aside.

Rinse the scallops under cold running water. If you are using sea scallops, cut them into thin strips; if you are using bay scallops, cut each one in half horizontally. Set the scallops aside.

Put 2 quarts of water on to boil in a large saucepan. Meanwhile, pour the tablespoon of safflower oil into a heavy-bottomed skillet over medium-low heat. When the oil is hot, add the scallops, lime juice and salt, and stir gently until the scallops turn pearl white — about one minute. Transfer the scallops to a bowl and refrigerate them until cool — at least 10 minutes.

Blanch the asparagus in the boiling water for 15 seconds; drain it and refresh it under cold running water. Transfer the asparagus to a plate lined with paper towels and refrigerate it.

To serve, drain the liquid from the scallops and gently toss them with the cold asparagus and the vinaigrette. Divide the mixture among individual plates; garnish each serving with a few orange sections.

EDITOR'S NOTE: *This dish is an ideal main course for a summer lunch. It may also be served as an appetizer at dinner.*

Broiled Sea Scallops in Champagne and Red Grape Sauce

Serves 4
Working time: about 15 minutes
Total time: about 35 minutes

Calories **215**
Protein **19g.**
Cholesterol **57mg.**
Total fat **7g.**
Saturated fat **4g.**
Sodium **235mg.**

1 lb. sea scallops, the bright white connective tissue removed
2 tbsp. unsalted butter
2 tbsp. finely chopped shallot
½ cup dry champagne or dry white wine
½ lb. seedless red grapes, cut in half (about 1½ cups), several whole grapes reserved for garnish
½ cup fish stock (recipe, page 136)
¼ tsp. salt
¼ tsp. white pepper
4 or 5 parsley sprigs (optional)

Melt 1 tablespoon of the butter in a saucepan over medium heat. Add the shallot and sauté it until it begins to color — about four minutes. Pour in all but 2 tablespoons of the champagne or white wine and continue to cook the mixture until the liquid is reduced by half — about five minutes. Add the grapes, stock, ⅛

teaspoon of the salt and ⅛ teaspoon of the pepper. Cook the mixture, stirring frequently, until nearly all the liquid has evaporated — about five minutes. Transfer the mixture to a blender or food processor and purée it. Strain the purée through a sieve into another saucepan. Stir the remaining wine into the sauce and set the sauce aside. Preheat the broiler.

Melt the remaining tablespoon of butter in a small skillet. Rinse the scallops under cold running water and pat them dry; season them with the remaining ⅛ teaspoon of salt and ⅛ teaspoon of pepper. Dip the two flat sides of each scallop into the melted butter and arrange the scallops in a single layer in a shallow flameproof casserole. Broil the scallops about 3 inches below the heat source for two minutes, then remove any that are considerably smaller than the others. Continue broiling the larger scallops for one minute more; turn them and broil them on the second side for one minute. Return the smaller scallops to the casserole, their cooked sides down, and broil all the scallops together until they are firm to the touch — two to three minutes.

Briefly reheat the sauce, then pour it into the bottom of a serving dish. Set the scallops on top of the sauce and garnish the dish with the reserved grapes and, if you wish, parsley sprigs.

SUGGESTED ACCOMPANIMENT: *rice tossed with fresh thyme.*

Ragout of Scallops and Red Peppers

Serves 4
Working (and total) time: about 45 minutes

Calories **225**
Protein **21g.**
Cholesterol **41mg.**
Total fat **8g.**
Saturated fat **1g.**
Sodium **250mg.**

1 lb. sea scallops, the bright white connective tissue removed
2 red peppers
freshly ground black pepper
1 tbsp. fresh lime juice
2 tbsp. red wine vinegar
2 tsp. fresh thyme, or ½ tsp. dried thyme leaves
2 tbsp. virgin olive oil
½ lb. mushrooms, wiped clean and quartered
¼ tsp. salt
½ cup dry white wine
1 bunch scallions, trimmed and cut into 1-inch-long pieces
2 Belgian endives (about ⅓ lb.), cut into 1-inch pieces, the pieces separated

Roast the peppers about 3 inches below a preheated broiler, turning them occasionally until they are blackened all over — about 15 minutes.

Meanwhile, rinse the scallops under cold running water. Cut the larger scallops in half. Put all the scallops in a bowl and sprinkle them with some black pepper. Stir in the lime juice and set the bowl aside.

Put the broiled peppers in a bowl and cover it with plastic wrap for one or two minutes (the trapped steam will loosen their skins). Working over the bowl to catch their juices, peel the peppers from top to bottom, then seed them. Coarsely chop the peppers and put them in a food processor or blender along with their reserved juices, the vinegar, thyme and some pepper; purée the mixture.

Pour the oil into a large, heavy-bottomed skillet over medium-high heat. When the oil is hot, add the mushrooms and sauté them for three minutes, stirring once. Sprinkle the mushrooms with ⅛ teaspoon of the salt, then pour in the wine. Continue cooking the mixture, stirring occasionally, until almost all of the liquid has evaporated — three to five minutes.

Pour the red-pepper purée into the skillet. Place the scallops on top and sprinkle them with some more black pepper and the remaining ⅛ teaspoon of salt. Cook the mixture for one minute, stirring frequently. Add the scallions and endives and continue cooking, stirring frequently, until the scallops are firm — two to three minutes more. Serve immediately.

SUGGESTED ACCOMPANIMENT: *steamed rice.*

Soft-Shell Clams with Prosciutto and Sage

Serves 4 as a first course
Working time: about 30 minutes
Total time: about 1 hour

Calories **115**
Protein **7g.**
Cholesterol **27mg.**
Total fat **4g.**
Saturated fat **2g.**
Sodium **130mg.**

2 lb. soft-shell clams, purged (technique, page 106)
¾ cup dry vermouth
1 oz. finely chopped prosciutto or other dry-cured ham
2 tbsp. finely chopped shallot
1 garlic clove, finely chopped
1 tbsp. chopped fresh sage, or 1 tsp. dried sage
freshly ground black pepper
2 tbsp. heavy cream
1 tbsp. finely chopped fresh parsley

Pour the vermouth into a large skillet or casserole. Bring the vermouth to a boil, then add the clams and cover the skillet. Cook the clams over high heat until they open — six to eight minutes. Discard any clams that remain closed. Do not pour out the cooking liquid.

Twist off and discard the top half of a clam shell. Slip a small, sharp knife under the clam and cut it free of the shell. Cut off the neck and set it aside. Return the clam to its half shell and set the shell in an ovenproof dish. Repeat these steps with the remaining clams. Cover the dish with aluminum foil and keep the clams warm in the oven.

Peel off and discard the blackish membrane covering the clam necks. Finely chop the clam necks.

Strain the clam-cooking liquid through a fine sieve into a smaller skillet over medium heat. Add the chopped clam necks along with the prosciutto, shallot, garlic, sage and some pepper. Cook the mixture until only about 2 tablespoons of liquid remain — approximately five minutes. Stir in the cream and bring the sauce to a simmer. Remove the clams from the oven. Stir the parsley into the sauce and spoon a little sauce over each clam. Serve immediately.

Clams with Orzo

Serves 4 as a main course, 6 as a first course
Working (and total) time: about 25 minutes

Calories **200**
Protein **12g.**
Cholesterol **34mg.**
Total fat **5g.**
Saturated fat **1g.**
Sodium **55mg.**

36 cherrystone or littleneck clams, scrubbed
½ cup orzo
1 tbsp. virgin olive oil
4 shallots, finely chopped
⅛ tsp. ground cinnamon
⅛ tsp. cayenne pepper
1 ripe tomato, peeled, seeded and chopped
¼ cup chopped fresh parsley

Tap the clams and discard any that will not close. Put the clams into a deep pot and pour 1 cup of water over them. Tightly cover the pot and set it over high heat. Steam the clams for five to eight minutes, periodically transferring the opened ones to a bowl. Discard any clams that remain closed.

Remove the clams from their shells and rinse them one by one in the cooking liquid in the pot to dislodge any clinging sand. Set the clams aside, and carefully pour the cooking liquid through a fine sieve into a medium saucepan, leaving behind as much sand as possible. Pour in 2 quarts of water and bring the liquid to a boil. Stir in the orzo and cook it until it is *al dente* — five to 10 minutes.

While the orzo is cooking, heat the oil in a large, heavy-bottomed skillet over medium heat. Add the shallots and cook them until they are translucent — about four minutes. Sprinkle in the cinnamon and cayenne pepper, and cook the mixture for 30 seconds. Add the tomato and parsley and cook the mixture for one minute more.

Drain the cooked orzo and stir it and the clams into the shallot-tomato mixture. Cook until the clams are heated through — one or two minutes.

Serve the clams and orzo in clam or scallop shells, in individual serving dishes or on a platter.

SUGGESTED ACCOMPANIMENT: *yellow squash sautéed with celery and thyme.*

Clams and Rice Yucatan Style

Serves 4
Working time: about 30 minutes
Total time: about 1 hour

Calories **470**
Protein **16g.**
Cholesterol **34mg.**
Total fat **8g.**
Saturated fat **1g.**
Sodium **200mg.**

36 littleneck clams, scrubbed
3 ripe tomatoes, peeled, seeded and coarsely chopped
1 large onion, coarsely chopped
3 garlic cloves, coarsely chopped
3 jalapeño peppers, seeded and coarsely chopped (caution, page 41)
2¼ cups fish stock (recipe, page 136) or water
2 tbsp. safflower oil
1½ cups rice
¼ tsp. salt
freshly ground black pepper
½ cup peas, blanched for 1 minute if fresh
juice of 1 lime
several fresh cilantro sprigs

Purée the tomatoes, onion, garlic, jalapeño peppers and ½ cup of the fish stock or water in a food processor or blender. Preheat the oven to 400° F.

Heat the oil in a large ovenproof skillet or casserole over medium heat. Add the rice and sauté it in the oil, stirring constantly, until it is lightly browned — three to four minutes. Stir in the tomato purée, the remaining 1¾ cups of stock or water, the salt and some black pepper. Bring the mixture to a simmer, reduce the heat to medium low and cook the rice, covered, until most of the liquid has been absorbed — about 15 minutes. Stir in the peas.

Tap the clams and discard any that do not close. Set the clams on top of the rice, cover the dish with aluminum foil and transfer it to the oven. Bake the clams until they open — about 10 minutes. Drizzle the lime juice over the clams and garnish the dish with the cilantro sprigs. Serve immediately.

SUGGESTED ACCOMPANIMENTS: *warm tortillas; raw jícama and orange salad or chopped avocado salad.*

Oysters with Julienned Vegetables in Basil-Butter Sauce

Serves 4 as a first course
Working (and total) time: about 30 minutes

Calories **220**
Protein **13g.**
Cholesterol **95mg.**
Total fat **9g.**
Saturated fat **4g.**
Sodium **325mg.**

20 large oysters, shucked (technique, page 135), the liquid reserved
3 tbsp. fresh lemon juice
1 large carrot, peeled and julienned
1 celery stalk, trimmed and julienned
1 leek, trimmed, split, washed thoroughly to remove all grit, and julienned
½ cup dry white wine
1 shallot, finely chopped
¼ tsp. salt
freshly ground black pepper
2 tbsp. fresh basil, Italian parsley or cilantro cut into thin strips
1½ tbsp. cold unsalted butter
1 lemon (optional), cut into wedges

Add 2 tablespoons of the lemon juice to 1 quart of water and bring the water to a boil. Drop the carrot julienne into the boiling water; after 30 seconds, add the celery julienne; after 15 seconds more, add the leek julienne. Cook the vegetables for an additional 15 seconds, then drain them and set them aside.

Pour the wine into a large, nonreactive skillet. Add the remaining lemon juice and the shallot, and bring the liquid to a simmer. Cook the liquid until it is reduced by half — about three minutes — and turn the heat to low. Lay the oysters in the skillet in a single layer; pour in the reserved juices and cook the oysters for 30 seconds. Turn the oysters over and cook them until they are heated through — about 30 seconds more. With a slotted spoon, transfer the oysters to warmed plates. Top each oyster with some of the julienned vegetables.

With the skillet still set over low heat, add the salt, some pepper and the basil. Whisk in the butter, then ladle some of the sauce over each oyster. Garnish the plates with lemon wedges, if you like, and serve the oysters immediately.

Peppery Oyster Seviche

Serves 6 as a first course
Working time: about 15 minutes
Total time: about 1 hour and 30 minutes

Calories **185**
Protein **8g.**
Cholesterol **45mg.**
Total fat **7g.**
Saturated fat **1g.**
Sodium **115mg.**

1 pint shucked small oysters
juice of 2 lemons
5 scallions, trimmed and finely chopped (about ½ cup)
juice of 2 limes
1½ tbsp. sweet chili sauce, or 1 tsp. hot red-pepper flakes mixed with 1 tbsp. corn syrup and 1 tsp. white vinegar
8 oz. fresh water chestnuts, peeled, sliced and blanched, or 8 oz. canned sliced water chestnuts, drained and rinsed
½ red pepper, seeded, deribbed and diced
¼ cup cilantro leaves
¼ cup finely chopped red onion
1 ripe avocado, peeled

Rinse the oysters under cold running water and cut them in half. In a bowl, combine the oysters with the lemon juice; let the oysters marinate at room temperature for one hour. When the oysters have marinated sufficiently, drain and discard the lemon juice. In another bowl, combine the scallions, lime juice, sweet chili sauce or red-pepper-flake mixture, water chestnuts, diced red pepper, cilantro and onion. Stir the mixture into the oysters. Cover the bowl and refrigerate it for 30 minutes.

Slice the avocado and arrange the slices in a sunburst pattern on a serving dish. Spoon the seviche onto the avocado and serve immediately.

The sauces that follow are designed to accompany oysters on the half shell; they may be presented alone or in concert. To avoid the risk of eating contaminated shellfish, be sure to purchase the oysters from a reliable fishmonger.

Red Wine Sauce

Serves 4
Working time: about 15 minutes
Total time: about 1 hour and 15 minutes

Calories **265**
Protein **14g.**
Cholesterol **95mg.**
Total fat **4g.**
Saturated fat **1g.**
Sodium **265mg.**

24 oysters, shucked (technique, page 135)
3 cups red wine
2 garlic cloves, finely chopped
2 tbsp. chopped shallot
1½ tbsp. fresh lemon juice
1 tsp. fresh thyme, or ¼ tsp. dried thyme leaves
2 tsp. honey
⅛ tsp. salt
freshly ground black pepper

Pour the wine into a nonreactive saucepan over medium heat. Cook the wine until it is reduced to 1 cup — about 20 minutes. Add the garlic, shallot, lemon juice, thyme, honey, salt and pepper, and cook for 10 minutes. Refrigerate the sauce for at least 45 minutes.

Herbed Yogurt Sauce

Serves 4
Working (and total) time: about 30 minutes

Calories **255**
Protein **17g.**
Cholesterol **131mg.**
Total fat **15g.**
Saturated fat **2g.**
Sodium **310mg.**

24 oysters, shucked (technique, page 135)
½ egg yolk
1 egg white
2 tbsp. safflower oil
1 tbsp. virgin olive oil
½ cup plain low-fat yogurt
2 scallions, trimmed and finely chopped
2 garlic cloves, very finely chopped
1½ tbsp. fresh lime juice
1 tsp. Dijon mustard
⅛ tsp. salt
freshly ground black pepper
1 tbsp. finely chopped fresh basil or Italian parsley, or 1 tbsp. finely cut fresh dill

Place the egg yolk and egg white in a large bowl. Whisking vigorously, pour the safflower oil into the bowl in a fine, steady stream. Incorporate the olive oil in the same way. Whisk in the yogurt, scallions, garlic, lime juice, mustard, salt, some pepper, and the basil, Italian parsley or dill. Refrigerate the sauce for at least 20 minutes to let the flavors meld.

Mignonette Sauce with Celery Seeds

Serves 4
Working (and total) time: about 25 minutes

Calories **110**
Protein **14g.**
Cholesterol **95mg.**
Total fat **4g.**
Saturated fat **1g.**
Sodium **195mg.**

24 oysters, shucked (technique, page 135)
¾ cup white wine vinegar
1 large shallot, very finely chopped
1 tsp. celery seeds
2 tbsp. finely chopped celery leaves
1 tsp. freshly ground black pepper

In a small bowl, whisk together the vinegar, shallot, celery seeds, celery leaves and pepper. Refrigerate the sauce until serving time.

Oysters in Red Wine with Mediterranean Herbs

Serves 4
Working time: about 20 minutes
Total time: about 45 minutes

Calories **240**
Protein **11g.**
Cholesterol **67mg.**
Total fat **10g.**
Saturated fat **2g.**
Sodium **200mg.**

1 pint shucked oysters, with their liquid
2 tbsp. virgin olive oil
10 shallots, finely chopped (about ½ cup)
4 garlic cloves, finely chopped
1 tsp. sugar
1 cup red wine
1 tsp. fresh rosemary, crushed, or ¼ tsp. dried rosemary
½ tsp. fennel seeds, crushed
1½ tsp. fresh thyme, or ½ tsp. dried thyme leaves
½ cup fresh bread crumbs
3 scallions, trimmed and finely chopped
freshly ground black pepper

Preheat the oven to 450° F.

Heat 1 tablespoon of the oil in a nonreactive sauce-pan over medium heat. Add the shallots and garlic, and cook them until they are translucent — about four minutes. Sprinkle in the sugar and cook, stirring con-stantly, until the shallots and garlic are golden brown — about three minutes more. Pour in the wine and season the sauce with half of the rosemary, ¼ tea-spoon of the fennel seeds and half of the thyme. Cook the sauce until only 1 tablespoon of liquid remains — about 10 minutes.

While the sauce is cooking, assemble the rest of the dish. In a small bowl, mix the remaining rosemary, fennel seeds and thyme with the bread crumbs, scal-lions and a generous grinding of pepper. Drain the oysters, reserving their liquid.

Pour the oyster liquid into the sauce, stirring well to dissolve any caramelized juices on the sides of the pan. Continue cooking the sauce until only ½ cup re-mains — about five minutes.

Combine the sauce with the oysters and spoon the mixture into an oiled gratin dish. Sprinkle the bread-crumb topping over the dish and drizzle the remaining tablespoon of oil over all.

Set the dish in the upper third of the oven and bake it until the top is lightly browned and the oysters are cooked — about 10 minutes. Serve at once.

SUGGESTED ACCOMPANIMENT: *zucchini sautéed with garlic.*

EDITOR'S NOTE: *Cooking the oyster mixture in four small gratin dishes makes for an equally attractive presentation.*

Spiced Oysters

Serves 8 as an hors d'oeuvre
Working time: about 5 minutes
Total time: about 6 hours

Calories **90**
Protein **10g.**
Cholesterol **67mg.**
Total fat **2g.**
Saturated fat **1g.**
Sodium **135mg.**

2 pints shucked oysters, the liquid reserved
2 tbsp. cider vinegar
½ tsp. grated nutmeg
¼ tsp. mace
⅛ tsp. cayenne pepper
9 whole cloves
½ tsp. sugar
5 whole allspice berries (optional)
2 heads Boston lettuce, the leaves washed and patted dry

Put the oysters and their liquid into a flameproof glass or earthenware dish. Add the vinegar, nutmeg, mace, cayenne pepper, cloves, sugar and allspice berries if you are using them; stir gently.

Fit a fireproof pad over a stove burner and set the dish with the oysters on the pad; turn the burner on to low. Heat the oysters very slowly until their edges curl and they are opaque — about 30 minutes.

Let the oysters cool slightly before refrigerating them for at least six hours. To serve, nestle each oyster in a lettuce leaf.

Crayfish Boil

Serves 4 as a first course
Working time: about 10 minutes
Total time: about 25 minutes

Calories **100**
Protein **19g.**
Cholesterol **179mg.**
Total fat **0g.**
Saturated fat **0g.**
Sodium **65mg.**

5 lb. live crayfish
4 onions, sliced
2 dried chili peppers
1 whole bulb of garlic, cut in half horizontally
⅓ cup fresh thyme, or 2 tbsp. dried thyme leaves
⅓ cup fresh rosemary, or 2 tbsp. dried rosemary
⅓ cup fresh sage, or 2 tbsp. dried sage
1 tbsp. dill seeds
1 tbsp. celery seeds
½ cup cider vinegar

To prepare the crayfish, immerse them in cold water for 10 minutes, then rinse the crayfish well under cold running water.

Pour 6 quarts of water into a large stockpot. Add the onions, chili peppers, garlic, thyme, rosemary, sage, dill seeds, celery seeds and vinegar, and bring the water to a boil. Add all the crayfish to the pot, tightly cover it, and return the water to a boil. Cook the crayfish for five minutes, then transfer them to a large platter. Serve the crayfish hot or cold, in their shells, and provide each guest with a liberal supply of paper napkins.

EDITOR'S NOTE: *The technique of eating boiled crayfish is easily mastered. Break the tail from the body, then split the tail shell lengthwise and remove the meat with your fingers. Crack the larger claws with your teeth and suck out the delicate morsel within.*

Chilled Crayfish and Shrimp with Spicy Sauce

Serves 8 as an hors d'oeuvre
Working time: about 35 minutes
Total time: about 1 hour and 45 minutes

Calories **105**
Protein **18g.**
Cholesterol **156mg.**
Total fat **1g.**
Saturated fat **0g.**
Sodium **140mg.**

5 lb. live crayfish, boiled (recipe, above), refrigerated in their cooking liquid for at least 6 hours
1 lb. medium shrimp, peeled and deveined
2 onions, sliced
1½ tsp. fresh thyme, or ½ tsp. dried thyme leaves
1 bay leaf
14 oz. canned unsalted tomatoes, chopped, the juice reserved
2 garlic cloves, finely chopped
½ tsp. sugar
¼ tsp. dried sage
¼ tsp. dill seeds
¼ tsp. celery seeds
¼ tsp. salt
⅛ tsp. cayenne pepper
juice of 1 lime
½ cup plain low-fat yogurt
2 scallions, trimmed and thinly sliced

Remove the crayfish from their cooking liquid and discard the liquid. Remove the tail meat from the shells and keep it chilled. Put all the shells (including the bodies, legs and claws) into a large pot along with the onions, half of the thyme and the bay leaf. Pour in enough water to cover the shells and bring the water to a boil. Cook the shells until the liquid remaining in the pot covers only half of them — about 20 minutes.

Strain the shell-cooking liquid into a saucepan and discard the solids. Bring the liquid to a simmer over medium heat. Add the shrimp and poach them until they turn opaque — approximately two minutes. Re-

move the shrimp from the liquid with a slotted spoon and chill them.

To obtain a concentrated crayfish essence, boil the cooking liquid until it is reduced to ½ cup — about 20 minutes. Set the liquid aside.

While the crayfish essence is reducing, prepare the dipping sauce. Combine the remaining thyme, the to- ▶

matoes and their juice, the garlic, sugar, dried sage, dill seeds, celery seeds, salt, cayenne pepper and lime juice in a saucepan. Bring the mixture to a boil and cook it over medium-high heat for 15 minutes, stirring frequently. Transfer the mixture to a blender or a food processor, and purée it until it is smooth. Return the mixture to the saucepan and cook it over medium heat until it becomes quite thick — approximately 10 minutes. Transfer the sauce to a bowl and allow it to cool thoroughly.

Stir 2 tablespoons of the crayfish essence into the sauce. (The remaining essence can be frozen in an ice-cube tray for later use in seafood sauces.) Mix in the yogurt and the scallions. Arrange the crayfish meat and the shrimp on a platter, and let each diner dip them into the sauce.

SUGGESTED ACCOMPANIMENT: *assorted raw vegetables.*

Lobster with Leek and Tomato Compotes

Serves 4
Working time: about 25 minutes
Total time: about one hour and 15 minutes

Calories **315**
Protein **30g.**
Cholesterol **104mg.**
Total fat **3g.**
Saturated fat **0g.**
Sodium **420mg.**

4 live lobsters (about 1¼ lb. each)
4 medium leeks, trimmed, split, washed thoroughly to remove all grit, the white parts sliced, the green leaves reserved
4 ripe tomatoes, peeled and seeded, the skins and seeds reserved, the flesh cut into strips about ¼ inch wide
1 tarragon sprig, the leaves removed from the stem, both reserved
8 peppercorns
1 cup dry white wine

Kill two of the lobsters by plunging them into a large pot of boiling water. Tightly cover the pot and boil the lobsters for one minute. Remove the lobsters with tongs and repeat the process with the remaining two lobsters. Pour out the water.

Working over the pot to catch the lobsters' juices, use the techniques demonstrated on pages 134 and 135 to remove the meat and the tomalley from each lobster. Cut the meat into 1-inch pieces and reserve it. Put all the shells, legs and tomalley into the pot. Add to the pot the leeks' green leaves, the tomato skins and seeds, the tarragon stem and the peppercorns. Pour in enough water to cover the shells, and bring the liquid to a boil. Cook the stock for 25 minutes.

Strain the stock into a large, heavy-bottomed skillet, discarding the solids. Boil the stock over high heat until it is reduced by half — about 10 minutes. Add the sliced leeks to the skillet and cook them until they are tender — about three minutes — then remove them with a slotted spoon and keep them warm. Pour in the wine and boil the liquid for three minutes more.

Spoon the lobster meat into the boiling liquid and cook it until it is opaque — about two minutes. Remove the lobster meat and keep it warm. Boil the liquid remaining in the skillet until it is reduced to 1 cup — about five minutes. Add the tomato strips and cook them, stirring gently, until they are heated through — about two minutes. Remove the tomato strips and toss them with the tarragon leaves.

Pour the sauce over the lobster and serve it with the leeks and tomatoes.

SUGGESTED ACCOMPANIMENT: *pappardelle, or other wide noodles.*

Stuffed Lobster

Serves 8
Working time: about 35 minutes
Total time: about 45 minutes

Calories **175**
Protein **16g.**
Cholesterol **52mg.**
Total fat **5g.**
Saturated fat **1g.**
Sodium **290mg.**

4 live lobsters (about 1¼ lb. each)
6 slices day-old white bread, crumbled into small pieces
2 tbsp. virgin olive oil
2 shallots, finely chopped, or ¼ cup finely chopped onion
¼ cup chopped fresh oregano, marjoram or Italian parsley
6 garlic cloves, finely chopped
freshly ground black pepper
⅓ cup fresh lemon juice
2 tsp. paprika, preferably Hungarian

To prepare the stuffing, combine the bread, oil, shallots, half of the oregano, half of the garlic and some pepper in a large bowl. Set the stuffing aside.

In a small bowl, combine the remaining oregano and garlic, the lemon juice, paprika and some pepper. Set the bowl aside.

Preheat the oven to 500° F.

Kill the lobsters by plunging them into a large pot of boiling water for one minute. Remove the lobsters with tongs and let them drain until they are cool enough to handle. Twist off the claws. Using a large, heavy knife, split each lobster down the entire length of the body and tail. Remove the tomalley with a spoon and chop it. Add the tomalley to the stuffing and mix well. Remove the viscera from the stomach cavity and discard them along with the thin side claws.

Arrange the lobster halves in a large baking dish with their cut sides up. Gently crack the claws (technique, page 135) and arrange them around the tails. Loosely fill the stomach cavities with the stuffing.

Drizzle the lemon-juice mixture over the tail meat only and place the baking dish in the oven. Bake the lobsters until the stuffing is lightly browned on top — 12 to 15 minutes.

Transfer the split lobsters (not the claws) to a large serving platter and cover them with aluminum foil to keep them warm. Return the claws to the oven and bake them for five minutes more. Arrange the claws around the lobsters and serve immediately.

SUGGESTED ACCOMPANIMENT: *cucumber-and-tomato salad.*

Lobster in Parsley-Cilantro Sauce

Serves 2
Working time: about 30 minutes
Total time: about 40 minutes

Calories **360**
Protein **30g.**
Cholesterol **104mg.**
Total fat **17g.**
Saturated fat **2g.**
Sodium **410mg.**

2 live lobsters (about 1¼ lb. each)
2 tbsp. virgin olive oil
¾ cup finely chopped onion
1 tsp. curry powder
½ tsp. turmeric
1 tbsp. fresh lemon juice
2 garlic cloves, finely chopped
freshly ground black pepper
1 ripe plum tomato, seeded and finely diced
1 cup coarsely chopped fresh parsley
¼ cup chopped cilantro

Pour enough water into a large pot to fill it about 1 inch deep. Bring the water to a boil, place the lobsters in the water and tightly cover the pot. Cook the lobsters until they turn pink — about 10 minutes. Remove the lobsters from the pot. When they are cool enough to handle, extract the meat from the tails and claws as shown on pages 134 and 135; reserve the shells.

Preheat the oven to 300° F. Return the lobster shells to the cooking pot and pour in 2 cups of water. Bring the water to a boil, reduce the heat to medium and simmer the shells for 10 minutes. Strain the liquid through a fine sieve into a saucepan and reduce it over medium heat until only about 1 cup remains — approximately 10 minutes.

While the lobster liquid is reducing, cut the tail meat of one of the lobsters into slices about ¼ inch thick. Arrange the slices in an overlapping pattern on an ovenproof serving plate, with the whole claw meat at the top, as in the photograph. Slice and arrange the other lobster on another plate in the same way. Cover the plates with foil and put them in the oven.

To prepare the sauce, pour the oil into a large skillet over medium-high heat. When the oil is hot, add the onion, curry powder and turmeric; cook the mixture, stirring frequently, until the onion is browned — about five minutes. Pour in the reduced lobster liquid, lemon juice, garlic and some pepper, and simmer the sauce for one minute. Stir in the tomato, parsley and half of the cilantro, and remove the skillet from the heat.

Remove the lobsters from the oven and lift off the foil. Pour half of the sauce around each lobster. Sprinkle the remaining two tablespoons of cilantro over the lobsters and serve them immediately.

SUGGESTED ACCOMPANIMENTS: *steamed asparagus and boiled new potatoes.*

Lobster and Penne with Marsala-Tomato Sauce

Serves 4
Working time: about 15 minutes
Total time: about 50 minutes

Calories **390**
Protein **22g.**
Cholesterol **52mg.**
Total fat **6g.**
Saturated fat **1g.**
Sodium **420mg.**

2 live lobsters (about 1¼ lb. each)
1 tbsp. safflower oil
1 small onion, finely chopped
2 garlic cloves, finely chopped
1 cup Marsala
2½ lb. ripe tomatoes, peeled, seeded and chopped, the juice reserved, or 28 oz. canned unsalted tomatoes, chopped, the juice reserved
2 tbsp. tomato paste
1 tbsp. chopped fresh oregano, or ½ tbsp. dried oregano
freshly ground black pepper
¼ tsp. salt
6 oz. penne or ditalini (about 2 cups)
4 or 5 oregano sprigs for garnish (optional)

Pour enough water into a large pot to fill it about 1 inch deep. Bring the water to a boil, place the lobsters in the water, and tightly cover the pot. Cook the lobsters until they turn red — about 10 minutes. Remove the lobsters from the pot and set them aside until they are cool enough to handle. Scoop out the tomalley, and extract the meat from the shells as shown on pages 134 and 135, reserving the larger pieces of shell. Cut the meat into 1-inch chunks and set it aside.

Heat the oil in a large casserole over medium heat. Add the onion and cook it, stirring occasionally, until it is translucent — about two minutes. Add the garlic and cook it for 30 seconds, then pour in the Marsala and add the reserved lobster shells. Cook the mixture until the wine is reduced by half — about two minutes. Add the tomatoes and their juice, the tomato paste, the tomalley, the oregano, some pepper and the salt. Partially cover the pot, and cook the sauce at a brisk simmer until the liquid is reduced by three quarters — about 20 minutes.

While the sauce is simmering, add the penne or ditalini to 2½ quarts of boiling water with 1 teaspoon of salt. Start testing the pasta after 10 minutes and cook it until it is *al dente*.

Remove the lobster shells from the sauce and discard them. Drain the penne and add it to the sauce, then add the lobster meat and cook the mixture over medium heat until it is heated through — about three minutes. Garnish the dish with the oregano sprigs if you wish, and serve immediately.

SUGGESTED ACCOMPANIMENT: *arugula salad.*

Grilled Shrimp with Tomato-Ginger Sauce

Serves 4
Working time: about 40 minutes
Total time: about 1 hour and 15 minutes

Calories **215**
Protein **17g.**
Cholesterol **130mg.**
Total fat **8g.**
Saturated fat **1g.**
Sodium **70mg.**

24 medium shrimp (about 1 lb.), peeled and deveined
1 onion, chopped
½ cup dry white wine
2 tbsp. fresh lemon juice
1 tbsp. virgin olive oil
Tomato-ginger sauce
1 tbsp. virgin olive oil
3 scallions, trimmed and chopped
6 garlic cloves, chopped
1 tbsp. finely chopped fresh ginger
2 jalapeño peppers, seeded and chopped (caution, page 41)
¼ tsp. ground coriander
¼ tsp. ground cumin
¼ tsp. dry mustard
3 ripe tomatoes, peeled, seeded and chopped
1 tsp. brown sugar
1 tbsp. red wine vinegar

In a bowl, combine the onion, wine, lemon juice and oil. Add the shrimp and let them marinate in the refrigerator for one hour.

Meanwhile, make the sauce. Pour the oil into a large, heavy-bottomed skillet over medium-high heat. When the oil is hot, add the scallions, garlic, ginger and jalapeño peppers; cook for two minutes, stirring constantly. Stir in the coriander, cumin and mustard, and cook the mixture for one minute more. Add the tomatoes and cook them, stirring constantly, for one minute. Remove the skillet from the heat and stir in the brown sugar and vinegar. Transfer the sauce to a serving bowl and let it cool.

Near the end of the marinating time, preheat the broiler. Thread the shrimp in interlocking pairs onto four skewers. Brush the shrimp with any remaining marinade and broil them about 2 inches below the heat source until they are opaque — approximately three minutes.

Serve the shrimp on their skewers atop a bed of rice, with the sauce presented alongside.

SUGGESTED ACCOMPANIMENTS: *steamed rice; chicory salad.*

Shrimp and
Green Bean Salad

Serves 4
Working time: about 30 minutes
Total time: about 1 hour

Calories **185**	1 lb. medium shrimp, the shells left on
Protein **20g.**	1½ lb. green beans, trimmed and cut in half
Cholesterol **133mg.**	1½ tbsp. tarragon vinegar
Total fat **6g.**	1 tbsp. safflower oil
Saturated fat **1g.**	2 tbsp. chopped fresh tarragon, or 2 tsp. dried tarragon
Sodium **235mg.**	2 tbsp. finely cut chives
	¼ tsp. salt
	freshly ground black pepper
	½ cup plain low-fat yogurt
	1 tbsp. sour cream
	1½ tsp. Dijon mustard
	1 tsp. tomato paste
	1 tbsp. chopped fresh parsley

Bring 8 cups of water to a boil in a large saucepan. Add the beans and boil them until they are just tender — about six minutes. Drain the beans and refresh them under cold running water. Pat the beans dry and trans-fer them to a bowl. Set the bowl aside.

Bring 4 cups of water to a simmer in the saucepan. Add the shrimp, cover the pan, and simmer the shrimp until they are opaque — two to three minutes. Drain the shrimp; when they are cool enough to handle, peel them (and, if you like, devein them). Add the shrimp to the beans.

In a small bowl, whisk together the vinegar, oil, half of the tarragon, 1 tablespoon of the chives, ⅛ teaspoon of the salt and some pepper. Arrange the shrimp and beans on a serving platter and spoon the vinegar-and-oil marinade over it. Let the dish marinate at room temperature for 30 minutes.

Near the end of the marinating time, prepare the dressing: Whisk together the yogurt, sour cream, mustard and tomato paste. Stir in the parsley, the other half of the tarragon and the remaining tablespoon of chives, the remaining ⅛ teaspoon of salt and some pepper. Pour the dressing into a small serving bowl and serve it alongside the salad.

SUGGESTED ACCOMPANIMENT: *whole-wheat pita bread.*

Sautéed Shrimp
with Sherry and Chilies

Serves 4
Working time: about 20 minutes
Total time: about 1 hour

Calories **140**	1 lb. shrimp, peeled and deveined if necessary, the shells reserved
Protein **16g.**	
Cholesterol **138mg.**	1 whole garlic bulb, the cloves separated and peeled
Total fat **4g.**	4 dried red chili peppers (caution, page 41)
Saturated fat **1g.**	1 tsp. fresh rosemary, or ½ tsp. dried rosemary
Sodium **55mg.**	½ tsp. fennel seeds
	⅓ cup dry sherry
	1 red pepper, seeded, deribbed and julienned
	1 scallion, trimmed and julienned
	1 tbsp. unsalted butter

Put the shrimp shells in a saucepan with the garlic, chili peppers, rosemary, fennel seeds and 1 quart of water. Bring the water to a boil, then reduce the heat to medium low and simmer the mixture for 30 minutes.

Strain the poaching liquid, discard the solids and return the liquid to the saucepan. Boil the liquid rapidly until only about 1½ cups remain — five to 10 minutes. Pour in the sherry and bring the liquid to a simmer. Poach the shrimp until they are opaque — approximately one minute. Remove the shrimp with a slotted spoon and set them aside.

Boil the remaining poaching liquid until only 2 or 3 tablespoons remain — about five minutes. Add the ju-

lienned red pepper, reduce the heat to medium, and cook the pepper for two minutes. Return the shrimp to the saucepan. Add the scallion and butter, and stir until the butter has melted and the shrimp are warm. Serve immediately.

SUGGESTED ACCOMPANIMENT: *steamed rice.*

EDITOR'S NOTE: *Served cold, this dish makes an ideal prelude to summer meals; olive oil or safflower oil should be used in place of the butter.*

Gingered Shrimp on Black Beans

Serves 6
Working time: about 1 hour
Total time: about 9 hours

Calories **425**
Protein **30g.**
Cholesterol **108mg.**
Total fat **6g.**
Saturated fat **1g.**
Sodium **345mg.**

1¼ lb. medium shrimp, peeled and deveined, the shells reserved
1-inch piece of fresh ginger, peeled and thinly sliced, plus 1 tbsp. chopped fresh ginger
1½ cups dry white wine
1 lb. dried black beans, soaked for at least 8 hours and drained
2 onions, chopped
4 garlic cloves, 2 crushed and 2 very thinly sliced
1 cinnamon stick, broken into 3 or 4 pieces
freshly ground black pepper
¼ tsp. salt
1 tbsp. grated lemon zest
2 tbsp. virgin olive oil
½ tsp. ground cinnamon
1 tsp. fresh lemon juice
3 scallions, trimmed and thinly sliced

Put the shrimp shells in a large saucepan. Add the ginger slices, 1 cup of the wine and 2 cups of water, and bring the mixture to a boil. Reduce the heat to medium and cook until the liquid is reduced by half — about 30 minutes. Strain the stock into a bowl, pressing down on the shells to extract any liquid, and set the bowl aside.

While the shells are cooking, put the drained beans in a large, heavy-bottomed saucepan along with the onions, crushed garlic cloves, the pieces of cinnamon stick and some pepper. Pour in enough water to cover the beans by about 1½ inches and boil the beans for 10 minutes. Skim off the foam and reduce the heat to low. Add the shrimp stock, salt and lemon zest, and simmer the mixture until the beans are tender but not mushy and a thick sauce results — one and a half to two hours. Remove the cinnamon-stick pieces and discard them.

About five minutes before the beans finish cooking, pour the oil into a large, heavy-bottomed skillet over medium-high heat. When the oil is hot, add the shrimp and sprinkle them with some pepper. Add the chopped ginger, the thinly sliced garlic and the ground cinnamon, and sauté the shrimp, stirring frequently, for three minutes. Pour the lemon juice and the remaining ½ cup of wine into the skillet; continue cooking the mixture, stirring frequently, until the shrimp are opaque and the liquid is reduced to a glaze — two to three minutes more. Stir in the scallions.

Pour the beans onto a serving platter and top them with the shrimp mixture. Serve immediately.

SUGGESTED ACCOMPANIMENT: *crisp green salad.*

Broccoli-Studded Shrimp

Serves 4
Working (and total) time: about 30 minutes

Calories **160**
Protein **17g.**
Cholesterol **130mg.**
Total fat **8g.**
Saturated fat **1g.**
Sodium **155mg.**

24 large shrimp (about 1¼ lb.), peeled, the tails left on
24 broccoli florets, each stem trimmed to 1 inch long and tapered to a point, blanched for 1 minute
2 scallions, trimmed and finely chopped
1 garlic clove, finely chopped
2 tsp. finely chopped fresh ginger
2 tbsp. rice vinegar
2 tbsp. rice wine or dry sherry
1 tsp. chili paste with garlic
1 tsp. tomato paste
1 tsp. cornstarch, mixed with 2 tbsp. water
2 tbsp. safflower oil

Using a skewer, make a ¼-inch-diameter hole through a shrimp from front to back, about one third of the way from its larger end. Insert a broccoli stem into the hole so that the floret nestles within the curve of the shrimp, as shown. Repeat the process with the remaining shrimp and broccoli. Carefully transfer the shrimp to a bowl with the scallions, garlic and ginger; toss the mixture gently and let it stand for 10 minutes.

While the shrimp are marinating, combine the vinegar, rice wine or sherry, chili paste, tomato paste and the cornstarch mixture in a small bowl. Stir the mixture well and set it aside.

Heat a wok or heavy-bottomed skillet over medium-high heat, then pour in the oil. Add half of the shrimp and gently stir fry them until they are opaque and firm — about two minutes. Remove the shrimp and keep them warm. Stir fry the second batch of shrimp.

Return the first batch of shrimp to the wok and pour in the sauce. Stirring gently to coat the shrimp, cook until the sauce thickens — about one minute.

SUGGESTED ACCOMPANIMENT: *rice with peppers and scallions.*

Seven-Spice Stew with Mussels, Squid and Shrimp

Serves 6
Working (and total) time: about 1 hour

Calories **165**
Protein **17g.**
Cholesterol **132mg.**
Total fat **2g.**
Saturated fat **0g.**
Sodium **265mg.**

1½ lb. mussels, scrubbed and debearded
½ lb. squid, cleaned and skinned (technique, page 132)
½ lb. medium shrimp, peeled and deveined if necessary
1 onion, chopped
1 cup dry white wine
2 ripe tomatoes, peeled, seeded and chopped
1 whole garlic bulb, the cloves peeled and thinly sliced
¼ tsp. ground turmeric
¼ tsp. ground cumin
¼ tsp. ground coriander
⅛ tsp. ground allspice
⅛ tsp. ground cloves
⅛ tsp. ground cardamom
⅛ tsp. cayenne pepper

Put the mussels in a deep pot, together with the onion and the wine. Cover the pot tightly and cook the mussels over medium-high heat until they open — about five minutes. Discard any mussels that remain closed. Let the mussels cool, then remove them from their shells and set them aside. Strain the mussel-cooking liquid into a bowl and let it stand for two or three minutes to allow any sand to settle out. Slowly pour most of the liquid into a large, heavy-bottomed skillet, leaving the sand behind.

Add the tomatoes, garlic and spices to the skillet. Bring the liquid to a boil, then reduce the heat to medium low and simmer the mixture until the garlic is tender — about five minutes.

Meanwhile, prepare the squid. Slit the pouches up one side and lay them flat on the work surface. Use a sharp knife to score a crosshatch pattern on the inside of each pouch. Cut the scored pouches into 1½-inch squares. Chop the tentacles into small pieces.

Add the squid to the liquid simmering in the skillet. Cover the skillet and cook the mixture until the squid pieces have curled up — about one minute. Add the shrimp, cover the pot and continue cooking until the shrimp are opaque — approximately one minute more. Finally, add the mussels and cook the stew for one minute to heat the mussels through. Serve at once.

SUGGESTED ACCOMPANIMENT: *couscous with raisins and almonds.*

Mussel Risotto

COOKING RICE BY THE REPEATED ADDITION OF LIQUID IS A TECHNIQUE PARTICULAR TO RISOTTO. IT RESULTS IN ESPECIALLY TENDER, MOIST RICE.

Serves 6
Working (and total) time: about 45 minutes

Calories **310**
Protein **20g.**
Cholesterol **87mg.**
Total fat **9g.**
Saturated fat **3g.**
Sodium **450mg.**

3 lb. mussels, scrubbed and debearded
1 tbsp. safflower oil
1 onion, finely chopped
1 cup long-grain rice
¼ cup dry white wine
8 to 10 saffron threads, crushed (about ⅛ tsp.)
1 cup small broccoli florets
1 tbsp. unsalted butter
½ cup freshly grated Parmesan cheese
¼ tsp. white pepper

Put the mussels in a large pot. Pour in ¼ cup of water, bring it to a boil, and tightly cover the pot. Steam the mussels until they open — five to six minutes. With a slotted spoon, transfer the opened mussels to a bowl; discard any that remain closed. Strain the mussel-cooking liquid through a fine sieve into a large measuring cup and set it aside.

Heat the oil in a flameproof casserole over medium heat. Add the onion and cook it, stirring occasionally, until it is translucent — two to three minutes. Add the rice and stir to coat it with the oil. Cook for one minute more. Pour in the wine and cook, stirring, until it has evaporated — about two minutes.

Strain into the measuring cup any liquid that has accumulated from the mussels. Add enough water to measure 1½ cups. Pour the liquid into the casserole and stir in the saffron. Bring the liquid to a boil, then reduce the heat to maintain a simmer. Cook the rice, stirring often, until it has absorbed most of the liquid — about 10 minutes.

Stir in 1 cup of hot water and continue to cook the rice, stirring, until the water is absorbed. Pour in a second cup of hot water; if necessary to maintain a very moist consistency, pour in an additional ½ cup of water. The rice is done when it is tender to the bite — 25 to 30 minutes.

While the rice is cooking, remove the mussels from their shells and set the mussels aside; discard the shells. Bring 1 quart of water to a boil in a saucepan. Add the broccoli and blanch it until it is barely tender — about two minutes. Drain the broccoli and refresh it under cold running water.

Melt the butter in a large, heavy-bottomed skillet over medium-high heat. Add the reserved mussels and broccoli florets, and sauté them until they are heated through — one to two minutes. Stir the cheese and pepper into the cooked rice, then stir in the mussels and broccoli; serve at once.

SUGGESTED ACCOMPANIMENT: *sliced Italian bread.*

Warm Mussel and Potato Salad

Serves 6
Working time: about 30 minutes
Total time: about 40 minutes

Calories **260**
Protein **18g.**
Cholesterol **76mg.**
Total fat **8g.**
Saturated fat **1g.**
Sodium **440mg.**

3 lb. mussels, scrubbed and debearded
1 tbsp. virgin olive oil
4 shallots, finely chopped
1 garlic clove, finely chopped
1 strip orange zest
¼ tsp. ground cumin
½ cup dry white wine
1 lb. boiling potatoes, peeled
¼ tsp. salt
¾ lb. radicchio or red-leaf lettuce, washed and dried
1 tbsp. cut chives

Chive-orange dressing

¼ cup fresh orange juice
1 tbsp. sherry vinegar or white wine vinegar
½ tsp. ground cumin
1 tbsp. virgin olive oil
1 cup plain low-fat yogurt
2 tbsp. finely cut chives
freshly ground black pepper

In a large, deep casserole, heat the olive oil over medium heat. Stir in the shallots, garlic, orange zest and cumin. Reduce the heat to low and cook the mixture, stirring occasionally, until the shallots are soft — five to seven minutes.

Pour in the wine and bring the liquid to a boil. Add the mussels, reduce the heat to medium, and cover the casserole. Cook the mussels until their shells have opened — five to six minutes. Discard any mussels that remain closed. Pour off the cooking liquid and set the mussels aside to cool.

While the mussels are cooking, put the potatoes in a saucepan, cover them with cold water, and sprinkle in the salt. Bring the water to a boil, cover the pan, and reduce the heat to medium. Cook the potatoes until they are tender — about 20 minutes. Drain them and set them aside until they are cool enough to slice.

To prepare the dressing, combine the orange juice, vinegar and cumin in a bowl. Slowly whisk in the oil, the yogurt, the 2 tablespoons of chives and a generous grinding of pepper.

Remove the mussels from their shells and transfer them to a clean bowl; add half of the dressing and toss well. Cut the potatoes into slices about ½ inch thick; toss the slices with the remaining dressing.

Lay the radicchio or lettuce around the edge of a large platter or individual plates. Arrange the potatoes

in an overlapping ring just inside the lettuce, then spoon the mussels into the center. Sprinkle the dish with the tablespoon of cut chives and serve.

SUGGESTED ACCOMPANIMENTS: *whole-wheat bread; goat cheese; fresh fruit.*

Steamed Mussels in Orange-Pernod Sauce

Serves 4
Working time: about 30 minutes
Total time: about 1 hour

Calories **275**	
Protein **22g.**	*36 large mussels, scrubbed, purged (box, page 106) and debearded*
Cholesterol **122mg.**	
Total fat **9g.**	*¾ cup fresh orange juice*
Saturated fat **3g.**	*¼ cup Pernod or other anise-flavored liqueur*
Sodium **480mg.**	*1 large, ripe tomato, peeled, seeded and chopped*
	½ cup chopped shallot
	2 garlic cloves, thinly sliced
	1 tsp. fresh thyme, or ¼ tsp. dried thyme leaves
	freshly ground black pepper
	1½ tbsp. cold unsalted butter, cut into small pieces

Put the orange juice, 2 tablespoons of the Pernod or other liqueur, the tomato, shallot, garlic, thyme and pepper into a large pot. Bring the mixture to a boil and add the mussels. Cover the pot tightly and steam the mussels, stirring once, until they open — five to six minutes. Discard any mussels that remain closed. Do not pour out the cooking liquid.

With a slotted spoon, transfer the mussels to a bowl, leaving the cooking liquid in the pot. Pour into the pot any juices that collect in the bowl, then cover the bowl with aluminum foil to keep the mussels warm while you finish the sauce. Quickly boil the liquid until it is reduced by half — three to four minutes. Reduce the heat to low; whisk in the butter, then the remaining 2 tablespoons of liqueur. Divide the mussels among four individual bowls. Pour the sauce over the mussels and serve them at once.

SUGGESTED ACCOMPANIMENT: *sour-dough dinner rolls.*

Preparing Mollusks for Cooking: To Purge or Not to Purge?

The notion of purging clams and mussels seems guaranteed to incite debate among cooks. Some feel that it is an essential first step, for it rids the shellfish of the sand they ingest while feeding and burrowing. Others maintain that the process rids them of flavor as well.

If you elect to purge mollusks, first scrub all debris from the outsides of their shells. Then place them in a bucket or the kitchen sink and cover them with several inches of cool water. Sprinkle half a cup of cornmeal into the water and let the clams or mussels stand for up to 30 minutes; the mollusks will take up the cornmeal and expel the sand or grit.

Mussels Stuffed with Spinach and Red Peppers

Serves 6 as a first course
Working time: about 40 minutes
Total time: about 1 hour

Calories **190**
Protein **15g.**
Cholesterol **73mg.**
Total fat **8g.**
Saturated fat **1g.**
Sodium **340mg.**

36 large mussels, scrubbed and debearded
2½ tbsp. virgin olive oil
6 shallots, finely chopped
4 garlic cloves, finely chopped
1 fresh thyme sprig, or ⅛ tsp. dried thyme leaves
½ cup dry white wine
2 red peppers
1 lb. spinach, stemmed and washed
⅓ cup chopped fresh parsley
freshly ground black pepper

Heat 1 tablespoon of the oil in a large, deep casserole over medium heat. Add one third of the shallots, half of the garlic, and the thyme. Cook the mixture until the

shallots are soft — three to five minutes. Pour in the wine, bring the liquid to a boil and add the mussels. Cover the casserole and cook the mussels until their shells have opened — five to six minutes. Discard any mussels that do not open. Strain the mussel-cooking liquid into a bowl. Reserve 2 tablespoons of the liquid and discard the rest. Set the mussels aside until they are cool enough to handle.

Preheat the broiler. While the mussels are cooking, broil the peppers about 3 inches from the heat source, turning them frequently, until they are blistered all over — 12 to 15 minutes. Put the peppers in a bowl and cover the bowl with plastic wrap (the trapped steam will loosen their skins); set the peppers aside to cool.

Working over the bowl, peel, then seed the peppers. Strain the juice and purée the peppers along with their juice and the reserved mussel liquid in a food processor or a blender. Set the purée aside.

Place the washed spinach, with just the water that clings to its leaves from washing, in a large pot over medium heat. Cover the pot and steam the spinach until it is wilted — one to two minutes. Transfer the spinach to a colander and set it aside.

To prepare the topping, heat the remaining 1½ tablespoons of oil in a small skillet over medium heat. Add the remaining shallots and garlic, and cook them until they are soft — three to five minutes. Stir in the parsley and black pepper and set the topping aside. Preheat the oven to 400° F.

Remove the mussels from their shells and reserve the mussels in a bowl. Discard half of the shells and separate the remaining shells at the hinge, for use in the presentation of the dish.

To stuff the mussels, place the empty half-shells on a large baking sheet. Line the inside of each shell with some spinach leaves. Spoon about 1 teaspoon of the red-pepper purée into each shell; top the purée with a mussel. Sprinkle the topping over the stuffed mussels.

Bake the mussels until they are quite hot — five to six minutes. Serve immediately.

Mussels with Green and Yellow Peppers

Serves 4 as a first course
Working time: about 20 minutes
Cooking time: about 50 minutes

Calories **110**
Protein **6g.**
Cholesterol **27mg.**
Total fat **8g.**
Saturated fat **1g.**
Sodium **255mg.**

24 large mussels, scrubbed and debearded
½ green pepper, seeded, deribbed and diced
½ yellow pepper, seeded, deribbed and diced
1 small ripe tomato, peeled, seeded and finely chopped
1 garlic clove, finely chopped
1 tbsp. finely chopped shallot
1 tbsp. balsamic vinegar or red wine vinegar
2 tbsp. safflower oil
⅛ tsp. salt
freshly ground black pepper
8 drops hot red-pepper sauce

Pour ¼ cup of water into a large pot. Add the mussels, cover the pot and bring the water to a boil. Steam the mussels until their shells open — four to five minutes. Transfer the opened mussels to a shallow dish. Discard any mussels that remain closed.

Working over the dish to catch the juices, remove the top shell from a mussel and discard it. Using a spoon, scoop beneath the mussel to sever the connective tissue that attaches the mussel to the bottom shell. Return the mussel to the shell and transfer it to a serving platter. Repeat the process to free the remaining mussels. Strain the collected mussel liquid through a fine sieve into a cup and set it aside.

Combine the peppers, tomato, garlic, shallot and vinegar in a small, nonreactive saucepan. Let the mixture stand for five minutes, then whisk in the oil, 1 tablespoon of the strained mussel liquid, the salt, some pepper and the hot red-pepper sauce. Bring the mixture to a simmer over medium heat and cook it for 30 seconds. Immediately spoon some of the mixture onto each mussel. Refrigerate the mussels, covered, for at least 30 minutes; serve them cold.

Squid Stewed in Red Wine

Serves 4
Working time: about 20 minutes
Total time: about 1 hour and 30 minutes

Calories **355**
Protein **21g.**
Cholesterol **266mg.**
Total fat **9g.**
Saturated fat **1g.**
Sodium **480mg.**

1½ lb. squid, cleaned and skinned (technique, page 132)
2 tbsp. virgin olive oil
¼ tsp. salt
3 medium leeks, trimmed, split, washed thoroughly to remove all traces of grit, and chopped
1 whole garlic bulb, the cloves separated and peeled (about 20 cloves)
1 lb. ripe plum tomatoes, peeled, seeded and chopped, or 14 oz. canned unsalted whole tomatoes, drained and chopped
1½ cups red wine
½ lb. zucchini, sliced into thin rounds
¼ cup basil or Italian parsley leaves, cut into thin strips
freshly ground black pepper

Heat ½ tablespoon of the olive oil in a large, heavy-bottomed skillet over medium-high heat. Add the squid and sauté it, stirring often, until it is opaque —
two to three minutes. Sprinkle ⅛ teaspoon of the salt on the squid and transfer the squid to a large, heavy-bottomed casserole.

Reduce the heat under the skillet to medium low. Pour 1 tablespoon of oil into the skillet, then add the leeks and garlic. Cover the skillet and cook, shaking the skillet occasionally to prevent the leeks and garlic from sticking, until they begin to turn golden brown — about 10 minutes. Transfer them to the casserole containing the squid. Add the tomatoes and wine, and bring the mixture to a boil. Reduce the heat to low, cover the casserole, and simmer the stew until the squid is tender — about one hour.

Pour the remaining ½ tablespoon of oil into the skillet over medium heat. Add the zucchini and cook it, stirring occasionally, until it is soft but not brown — about three minutes. Sprinkle the zucchini with the remaining ⅛ teaspoon of salt and transfer it to a bowl.

Before serving the stew, add the softened zucchini, the basil or Italian parsley, and some pepper; stir gently to mix them in, and serve immediately.

SUGGESTED ACCOMPANIMENT: *vermicelli or thin spaghetti tossed with fresh herbs.*

Rice-Stuffed Squid

Serves 4
Working time: about 45 minutes
Total time: about 1 hour

Calories **410**
Protein **19g.**
Cholesterol **224mg.**
Total fat **8g.**
Saturated fat **1g.**
Sodium **445mg.**

4 medium squid (about 1¼ lb.), cleaned and skinned (technique, page 132), the body pouches left whole, the tentacles finely chopped
¾ cup glutinous rice
1 cup dry white wine
1 tbsp. sugar
4 scallions, trimmed and sliced into thin rounds
1 garlic clove, finely chopped
1 tsp. finely chopped fresh ginger
1 tbsp. low-sodium soy sauce
1 tbsp. rice vinegar
2 tbsp. safflower oil
freshly ground black pepper
1 carrot, peeled and grated
½ cup peas
1 tbsp. prepared horseradish

Bring 1½ cups of water to a boil in a saucepan. Add the chopped squid tentacles and the rice; stir, reduce the heat to low and tightly cover the pan. Cook the mixture until most but not all of the liquid has been absorbed — 15 to 20 minutes.

While the rice is cooking, make the sauce. Put the wine and sugar into a nonreactive saucepan. Rapidly boil the mixture until it is reduced by half — about four minutes. Remove the pan from the heat and stir in half of the scallions, the garlic, ginger, soy sauce, vinegar, 1 tablespoon of the oil and some pepper. Pour the sauce into a small bowl.

Stir the carrot and peas into the rice. Cover the pan and cook the mixture until all the liquid has been absorbed and the rice is sticky and tender — about five minutes. Transfer the rice mixture to a bowl. Stir in the remaining scallions, the horseradish and a generous grinding of black pepper.

Preheat the broiler. Stuff the squid pouches with the rice mixture, leaving ½ inch unfilled at the open end. Secure the ends with wooden picks. Wipe off the outsides of the pouches, brush them with the remaining tablespoon of oil and set them on a broiler pan.

Broil the stuffed squid about 4 inches below the heat ▶

source for 10 minutes, giving them a quarter turn every two to three minutes. Allow the squid to stand for a minute or two before slicing them for serving. Pass the sauce separately.

SUGGESTED ACCOMPANIMENT: *steamed spinach with sesame seeds.*

EDITOR'S NOTE: *Glutinous rice, a round-grain rice that becomes sticky when cooked, can be found in Asian groceries. Because the amount of liquid it absorbs during cooking can vary, you may need to add more water as the rice cooks.*

Stir-Fried Squid with Asparagus and Mushrooms

Serves 4
Working time: about 35 minutes
Total time: about 45 minutes

Calories **230**
Protein **20g.**
Cholesterol **265mg.**
Total fat **8g.**
Saturated fat **1g.**
Sodium **565mg.**

1½ lb. squid, cleaned (technique, page 132)
8 dried Asian mushrooms, covered with 1 cup boiling water and soaked for 20 minutes
2 tbsp. rice wine
2 garlic cloves, finely chopped
2 tbsp. safflower oil
½ lb. asparagus, trimmed and sliced diagonally into 1½-inch lengths
4 scallions, trimmed and thinly sliced diagonally
1 tbsp. low-sodium soy sauce
1 tbsp. rice vinegar
1 tbsp. fermented black beans, rinsed and mashed
2 tsp. cornstarch

Remove the mushrooms from their soaking liquid and set them aside. Carefully pour the liquid into a small saucepan, leaving behind any grit. Boil the mushroom-soaking liquid until it is reduced to ¼ cup — about five minutes. Set the pan aside.

While the liquid is reducing, stem the mushrooms and slice each one into quarters.

Slit the squid pouches and then flatten them out on a work surface. With a sharp knife, score the inside surface of each pouch in a crosshatch pattern. Cut the pouches into 1-inch squares. Combine the squares and the tentacles with the rice wine and the garlic. Marinate the squid in this mixture for 15 minutes at room temperature.

Drain the squid, reserving the marinade. Heat 1 tablespoon of the safflower oil in a wok or a large, heavy-bottomed skillet over high heat. Add half of the squid pieces and stir fry them until the squares are tightly curled — about two minutes. Remove and reserve the squid. Heat ½ tablespoon of the remaining oil in the wok or skillet and stir fry the second batch of squid; set it aside with the first.

Heat the remaining ½ tablespoon of oil in the wok or skillet. Add the mushrooms, asparagus and scallions, and stir fry them for two minutes. Add the soy sauce, vinegar, fermented black beans and the reserved marinade, and cook the mixture for one minute longer.

Combine the reduced mushroom-soaking liquid and the cornstarch, and pour the mixture into the wok or skillet. Stir the vegetables until the sauce has thickened. Combine the squid with the vegetables and stir a few times to heat the squid through. Serve at once.

SUGGESTED ACCOMPANIMENT: *Asian wheat noodles or brown rice.*

Octopus with Yellow Peppers

Serves 4
Working time: about 30 minutes
Total time: about 2 hours

Calories **310**
Protein **27g.**
Cholesterol **209mg.**
Total fat **5g.**
Saturated fat **1g.**
Sodium **540mg.**

4 small octopuses (or squid), about 12 oz. each
juice of 1 lemon
3 bay leaves, broken in half
2 ripe tomatoes, seeded and coarsely chopped
1 tbsp. virgin olive oil
2 garlic cloves, thinly sliced
¼ tsp. salt
freshly ground black pepper
2 onions, thinly sliced
2 yellow or green peppers, seeded, deribbed and sliced lengthwise into strips about ¼ inch wide
2 cups red wine

Rinse the octopuses under cold running water and pat them dry with paper towels. Lay out each octopus to its full length and sever the tentacles from the head just below the eyes, as demonstrated below. Discard the heads. Remove the skin from the area above the tops of the tentacles, then separate the tentacles.

Put the octopus tentacles, lemon juice and bay leaves in a large nonreactive casserole or pot over medium heat. Cover the pan tightly and cook the tentacles for 15 minutes, stirring once (the tentacles will exude enough juice to provide a cooking liquid).

Add the tomatoes, oil, garlic, salt and some black pepper to the casserole, and stir well. Add the onions and yellow or green peppers, then pour the wine over all, stirring gently. Bring the liquid to a simmer. Cook the mixture, stirring occasionally, until the octopus is tender — 40 to 50 minutes. Remove the casserole from the heat and let it stand for about 30 minutes so that the flavors can mingle. Remove the bay leaves and reheat the dish briefly before dividing it among individual serving bowls.

SUGGESTED ACCOMPANIMENT: *orzo or rice.*

Preparing an Octopus for Cooking

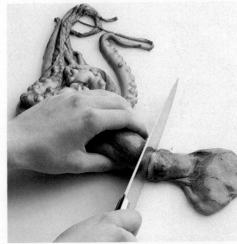

SEVERING THE HEAD. Rinse the octopus in cold water and lay it on a work surface. Place a knife below the eyes and slice the head from the tentacles. If the beak is still attached to the tentacle section, squeeze it out. Peel the skin from the area just above the base of the tentacles. Discard the head, beak and skin.

4 *Cooked in minutes, mussels, scallops, shrimp and stone-crab claws are served in a broth seasoned with saffron, fennel seeds and thyme (recipe, opposite).*

Microwaving Fish and Shellfish

Freshness of flavor, high nutritional value, speedy preparation — these beneficent basics of fish and shellfish cookery get an extra boost from the microwave oven. Furthermore, even the leanest specimens retain their moisture. Since extra liquid is seldom needed, no vitamins or minerals are lost in the cooking medium.

Fish steaks and fillets make the best candidates for microwaving; their uniform texture and shape allow them to cook evenly. For best results, place the thicker portions toward the outside of the dish or overlap the thinner sections in a wreathlike fashion. Then cover the dish with heavy-duty plastic wrap and set the oven on high power. The results are similar to conventional steaming or poaching.

Shellfish also cook to advantage in the microwave oven. Shrimp and shucked scallops, oysters and clams need only two to three minutes a pound; however, they should be stirred halfway through the process. A whole lobster steams in eight to 10 minutes. Whole crabs, on the other hand, cook unevenly because of their shape and numerous appendages; picked crab meat presents no problem.

The microwave oven even offers an easy way to open stubborn clams or oysters. Simply arrange the mollusks in a dish with their hinges facing out and cover them. Microwave on high power until the shells have opened just slightly.

The 17 recipes in this chapter have been tested in 625-watt and 700-watt ovens; the term "high" is used to indicate full power. To avoid overcooking, check fish and shellfish for doneness after the shortest time specified. Remember that food continues to cook briefly after it has left the microwave. Fish should still be slightly translucent in the center when removed from the oven. Set the dish aside for three to five minutes, and it will be done to a perfect turn.

Shellfish Cioppino

THIS RECIPE IS A FRESH ADAPTATION OF THE TRADITIONAL CIOPPINO, A FISH STEW INTRODUCED BY ITALIAN SETTLERS IN CALIFORNIA.

Serves 4
Working time: about 20 minutes
Total time: about 50 minutes

Calories **210**
Protein **21g.**
Cholesterol **91mg.**
Total fat **5g.**
Saturated fat **2g.**
Sodium **340mg.**

4 stone crab claws or Dungeness crab claws
12 mussels, scrubbed and debearded
½ lb. sea scallops, the bright white connective tissue removed, the scallops rinsed and patted dry
8 large shrimp (about ¼ lb.), peeled (the tails left on) and deveined
1 tbsp. unsalted butter
2 garlic cloves, finely chopped
1 medium leek, trimmed, split, washed thoroughly to remove any grit, and chopped
1 ripe tomato, peeled, seeded and chopped (about ½ cup)
2 cups fish stock (recipe, page 136)
1 cup dry vermouth
10 saffron threads, crushed
¼ tsp. fennel seeds
½ tsp. fresh thyme, or ¼ tsp. dried thyme leaves
¼ tsp. salt
freshly ground black pepper

Put the butter in a bowl, cover it with plastic wrap or a lid, and microwave it on high until the butter is melted — 40 seconds. Add the garlic and the leek, and stir to coat them with the butter. Cover the bowl again and cook the mixture on medium high (70 percent power) for two minutes, stirring once halfway through the cooking time.

Add the tomato, stock, vermouth, saffron, fennel seeds, thyme, salt and some pepper to the bowl; then cover it and microwave the contents on high for seven minutes. Uncover the bowl and cook the mixture until it is reduced by one third — about 15 minutes more.

While the stock mixture is cooking, twist each crab claw at the first joint to break off the pincer segment. With a nutcracker, crack each pincer segment across its thickest part (technique, page 133). Remove the part of the shell between the crack and the open end ▶

of the segment, leaving the claw meat in place; this makes the meat easier to remove at the table. Crack the other claw segments, remove and reserve the meat, and discard the shells.

When the stock mixture is reduced, remove it from the oven and set it aside. Put the mussels in a bowl and cover the bowl with plastic wrap or a lid. Microwave the mussels on high until they begin to open — about two minutes. Remove the mussels that have opened and set them aside in their shells; discard any unopened mussels.

Put the reserved crab meat, the crab claws, the scallops, and shrimp in the bowl with the stock mixture. Cover the bowl and microwave the shellfish on high for two minutes. Stir the shellfish to rearrange them, then add the mussels, spooning some of the liquid over them. Cook the stew on high until all the shellfish are cooked through — about 90 seconds more. Serve the cioppino piping hot.

SUGGESTED ACCOMPANIMENT: *salad of romaine lettuce leaves and radishes.*

Orange-Ginger Trout

Serves 8
Working time: about 30 minutes
Total time: about 1 hour

Calories **250**
Protein **28g.**
Cholesterol **83mg.**
Total fat **10g.**
Saturated fat **2g.**
Sodium **155mg.**

4 trout, about 1 lb. each, filleted (technique, page 130) and skinned (about 2 lb. of fillets)
2 oranges, the grated zest and juice of 1 reserved, the other left whole
1 tbsp. finely chopped fresh ginger
2 shallots, finely chopped
1 cup dry white wine
2 lb. spinach, washed and stemmed
1 garlic clove, finely chopped
¼ tsp. salt
freshly ground black pepper
1 tbsp. unsalted butter

Rinse the fillets under cold running water and pat them dry with paper towels. In an 8-inch-round baking dish,

combine the grated orange zest, orange juice, ginger, shallots and wine. Place the fillets in the liquid and let them marinate at room temperature for 30 minutes.

Put half of the spinach, with the water still clinging to it, and half of the garlic in a bowl, and microwave them on high for three minutes. Repeat the process to cook the remaining spinach and garlic; set both of the batches aside.

Meanwhile, peel and section the whole orange, and remove the outer membrane from each segment.

Remove the fillets from their marinade. Fold each fillet loosely in thirds, with the boned side out and the ends tucked under the middle, as you would a business letter. Add the salt and some pepper to the marinade and stir it well. Replace the folded fillets in the marinade, with their sides not touching, and microwave them on high until they are slightly translucent — five to seven minutes. Remove the fillets from the cooking liquid and set them aside.

Strain the liquid into a small bowl and microwave it on high, uncovered, until it is reduced by half — about five minutes. Add the butter and cook the mixture for two minutes more.

Arrange the spinach in an even layer in the baking dish. Place the folded fillets on the spinach bed and top each one with an orange segment. Return the dish to the oven and microwave it on high until it is warmed through — about 90 seconds. Pour the sauce over all and serve immediately.

SUGGESTED ACCOMPANIMENT: *lettuce-and-tomato salad.*

Scallop-and-Shrimp Brochettes

Serves 4
Working (and total) time: about 15 minutes

Calories **95**
Protein **17g.**
Cholesterol **77mg.**
Total fat **1g.**
Saturated fat **0g.**
Sodium **230mg.**

½ lb. sea scallops, the bright white connective tissue removed, the scallops rinsed and halved horizontally
½ lb. medium shrimp, peeled and deveined
1 tbsp. low-sodium soy sauce
juice of 1 lime
½ tsp. honey

Combine the soy sauce, lime juice and honey in a small bowl. Thread the scallops and shrimp onto wooden skewers (do not use metal). Brush the brochettes with half of the sauce.

Set the brochettes on a microwave roasting rack or in a baking dish and cook them on high for four minutes, turning them over midway through the cooking. Brush the brochettes with the remaining sauce and serve them at once.

SUGGESTED ACCOMPANIMENT: *spaghetti squash tossed with diced red pepper and dark sesame oil.*

Warm Scallop Salad with Cilantro Sauce

Serves 4
Working time: about 25 minutes
Total time: about 45 minutes

Calories **70**
Protein **10g.**
Cholesterol **21mg.**
Total fat **1g.**
Saturated fat **0g.**
Sodium **125mg.**

½ lb. sea scallops, the bright white connective tissue removed, the scallops rinsed and halved horizontally
juice of 1 lemon
juice of 1 lime
6 cilantro sprigs, the stems and leaves chopped separately
½ tsp. brown sugar
⅛ tsp. salt
⅛ tsp. cayenne pepper
1 head Belgian endive, the leaves separated, washed and dried
1 head Boston lettuce, the leaves separated, washed and dried
2 cherry tomatoes, thinly sliced

Put the scallops, lemon juice, lime juice and chopped cilantro stems in a shallow baking dish. Let the scallops marinate in the refrigerator for 30 minutes.

At the end of the marinating time, tightly cover the dish with heavy-duty plastic wrap and microwave the scallops on high for two minutes. Let the dish stand for one minute and then remove the scallops from the marinade; set them aside on a plate. Strain the marinade into a glass bowl; discard the cilantro stems.

To make the dressing, add the sugar, salt and cayenne pepper to the strained marinade. Microwave the liquid on high until it is reduced to about ¼ cup — five to six minutes.

Arrange the endive, lettuce and tomatoes on individual plates. Stir the chopped cilantro leaves and the scallops into the dressing. Reheat the scallops in the dressing for one minute on high. Transfer the scallops and dressing to the plates, and serve at once.

Hake Timbales with Tomato-Jalapeño Sauce

Serves 8 as a first course
Working (and total) time: about 45 minutes

Calories **110**
Protein **12g.**
Cholesterol **19mg.**
Total fat **3g.**
Saturated fat **1g.**
Sodium **170mg.**

1 lb. hake fillets (or cod), rinsed, patted dry and finely chopped
2 onions, finely chopped
2 jalapeño peppers, seeded and finely chopped (caution, page 41)
2 tsp. finely chopped lime zest
1 tbsp. chopped fresh oregano, or ½ tsp. dried oregano
1 tbsp. virgin olive oil
½ cup fresh bread crumbs
½ cup skim milk
½ cup plain low-fat yogurt
2 egg whites
⅛ tsp. salt
8 oregano or parsley sprigs (optional)

Tomato-jalapeño sauce
3 ripe tomatoes, peeled, seeded and chopped, or 14 oz. canned unsalted whole tomatoes, drained and chopped
2 jalapeño peppers, seeded and finely chopped (caution, page 41)
1 tbsp. chopped fresh oregano, or ½ tsp. dried oregano
1 tsp. red wine vinegar
⅛ tsp. salt

In a small bowl, stir together the onions, jalapeño peppers, lime zest, oregano and oil. Cover the bowl with plastic wrap or a lid and microwave it on high for four minutes, stirring the mixture halfway through the cooking time. Set the bowl aside for two minutes.

In a 2-quart bowl, combine the bread crumbs, milk and yogurt. Add the fish and the onion mixture; stir well, then add the egg whites and salt. Beat the mixture until it comes away from the sides of the bowl.

Spoon the fish mixture into eight lightly oiled 4-ounce ramekins. Cover the ramekins individually with plastic wrap, then microwave them on high for eight minutes, stopping after four minutes to rotate each one a half turn. Remove the timbales from the oven and let them stand while you prepare the sauce.

Combine the sauce ingredients in a bowl and stir well. Turn the timbales out onto plates. Ladle some of the sauce around the timbales and pour the remaining sauce into its own serving bowl. Garnish each plate with the oregano or parsley sprigs if you wish, and serve immediately.

Soused Perch

SOUSED (PICKLED) FISH CAN BE MADE UP TO 24 HOURS IN ADVANCE AND REFRIGERATED. ITS FLAVOR IMPROVES WITH TIME.

Serves 8 as a first course
Working time: about 20 minutes
Total time: about 1 hour and 20 minutes

Calories **65**
Protein **11g.**
Cholesterol **24mg.**
Total fat **2g.**
Saturated fat **0g.**
Sodium **65mg.**

1 lb. ocean perch fillets (or fresh herring), skin left on
1 small onion, sliced, the rings separated
1 small carrot, quartered lengthwise and sliced
1 bay leaf
½ tsp. coriander seeds
¼ tsp. mustard seeds
¼ tsp. celery seeds
8 black peppercorns
¼ cup cider vinegar
¼ tsp. salt

In a 12-inch round glass dish, combine the onion, carrot, bay leaf, coriander seeds, mustard seeds, celery seeds and peppercorns with 1 cup of water. Cover the plate with plastic wrap or a lid and microwave it on high for three minutes. Rotate the dish half a turn and cook the contents for two minutes more. Remove the plate from the oven and let it stand for three minutes.

Add the vinegar and salt to the mixture and stir gently to dissolve the salt. Rinse the fillets under cold running water. Place the fillets in the dish, with their skin sides up and their edges not touching. Cook the fish on high, uncovered, for two minutes. Turn the plate half a turn and cook until the fish feels firm to the touch — one or two minutes more. Refrigerate the fish, in its liquid, for at least one hour. Serve the soused fish chilled or at room temperature.

SUGGESTED ACCOMPANIMENT: *pumpernickel bread.*

Salmon Steaks in Three-Pepper Stew

Serves 4
Working time: about 30 minutes
Total time: about 45 minutes

Calories **310**
Protein **25g.**
Cholesterol **90mg.**
Total fat **18g.**
Saturated fat **4g.**
Sodium **155mg.**

4 salmon steaks, about 5 oz. each
2 lb. ripe tomatoes, peeled, seeded and chopped
2 red peppers, seeded, deribbed and cut into ¼-inch-wide strips
2 green peppers, seeded, deribbed and cut into ¼-inch-wide strips
2 jalapeño peppers, finely chopped (caution, page 41)
2 garlic cloves, finely chopped
1 tbsp. chopped fresh marjoram, or 1 tsp. dried marjoram
⅛ tsp. salt
freshly ground black pepper
1 tbsp. virgin olive oil
juice of 1 lime

Put the chopped tomatoes in a fine sieve and set them aside to drain for at least 30 minutes.

While the tomatoes are draining, remove the skin from the salmon steaks with a small, sharp knife. Divide each steak into two boneless pieces by cutting down each side of the backbone and around the ribs. Reassemble each steak as shown in the photograph, with the skinned sides facing out, the thicker parts interlocking, and the tapered flaps wrapped around the whole. Put the steaks in a baking dish, cover it tightly with heavy-duty plastic wrap and set it aside.

In a second baking dish, combine the red, green and jalapeño peppers with the garlic, marjoram, salt, some black pepper and 1 teaspoon of the oil. Cover the dish tightly and microwave the contents on high for four minutes, stirring once midway through the cooking time. Remove the pepper stew from the oven and let it stand while you cook the fish.

Microwave the fish on high, rotating the dish half a turn after two minutes, until the fish is slightly translucent — about four minutes in all. Let the fish stand while you prepare the tomato sauce. Put the drained tomatoes in a small bowl with the lime juice and the remaining 2 teaspoons of oil, and stir the mixture well.

Serve the salmon steaks surrounded by the pepper stew with the fresh tomato sauce on the side.

SUGGESTED ACCOMPANIMENT: *French bread.*

Clams on the Half Shell with Lemon-Thyme Sauce

Serves 4 as a first course
Working (and total) time: about 30 minutes

Calories **125**	24 cherrystone clams, scrubbed
Protein **8g.**	1 cup dry white wine
Cholesterol **45mg.**	1 shallot, finely chopped
Total fat **5g.**	1 tsp. fresh thyme, or ¼ tsp. dried thyme leaves
Saturated fat **3g.**	2 garlic cloves, finely chopped
Sodium **50mg.**	2 tbsp. fresh lemon juice
	1½ tbsp. cold unsalted butter, cut into small pieces
	3 tbsp. chopped fresh parsley
	freshly ground black pepper

Tap the clams and discard any that do not close. Arrange 12 of the clams in a circle on a large plate, with their hinges facing outward. Microwave them on high, turning the plate a half turn midway through the cooking, until they barely open — about five minutes. (They will not be cooked through.) Remove the clams and cook a second batch of 12 in the same manner.

While the clams are cooking, put the wine, shallot and thyme in a saucepan on the stove. Boil the mixture over medium heat until only about ⅓ cup of liquid remains — approximately seven minutes. Stir in the garlic and lemon juice. Reduce the heat to low to keep the sauce warm.

Slide the blade of a small knife inside a clam shell at a point opposite the hinge. Twist the blade to force the halves apart, then slide the blade along the inside of a half shell to sever the tough muscles that hold the shell closed. Twist off the freed half shell and discard it. Run the blade under the clam to free it, but leave it in the shell. Set the clam on a serving plate. Repeat these steps with the remaining clams.

Remove the sauce from the heat and whisk in the butter, then the parsley and pepper. Transfer the sauce to a small bowl and serve it alongside the clams.

Shrimp Teriyaki

Serves 4
Working time: about 20 minutes
Total time: about 30 minutes

Calories **125**
Protein **17g.**
Cholesterol **130mg.**
Total fat **1g.**
Saturated fat **0g.**
Sodium **405mg.**

1 lb. shrimp, peeled and deveined
¼ cup sweet sherry
2 tbsp. low-sodium soy sauce
1 tsp. rice vinegar
1 garlic clove, finely chopped
1 slice whole-wheat bread
1 tsp. cornstarch
½ cup fish stock (recipe, page 136) or dry white wine
1 carrot, peeled and julienned
3 scallions, trimmed and cut into 2-inch pieces, the pieces thinly sliced lengthwise

Combine the sherry, soy sauce, vinegar and garlic in a bowl. Add the shrimp and stir gently to coat them evenly. Marinate the shrimp in the refrigerator for 20 minutes, stirring them from time to time.

Microwave the slice of bread on high for two minutes. Place the bread in a plastic bag and crush it into crumbs with a rolling pin.

Mix the cornstarch with 1 tablespoon of the stock or wine. Strain the marinade into a glass bowl; stir in all but 2 tablespoons of the remaining stock or wine, along with the cornstarch mixture. Microwave this sauce on high for three minutes. Stir the sauce until it is smooth, then set it aside.

Dip the shrimp into the bread crumbs to coat them on one side. Arrange the shrimp, coated side up, in a shallow dish. Pour in the remaining 2 tablespoons of stock or wine. Cover the dish with plastic wrap or a lid, and microwave it on high for three minutes. Rearrange the shrimp, turning any uncooked pieces toward the edge of the dish.

Stir the carrot and scallion strips into the sauce; pour the sauce around the shrimp. Cover the dish again and cook it on medium high (70 percent power) for two minutes. Allow the shrimp to stand, covered, for another two minutes before transferring them to a serving dish. Spoon the sauce and vegetables around the shrimp and serve immediately.

SUGGESTED ACCOMPANIMENT: *stir-fried rice.*

Mussels in Peppery Red-Wine Sauce

Serves 4 as a first course
Working (and total) time: about 15 minutes

Calories **165**
Protein **14g.**
Cholesterol **73mg.**
Total fat **6g.**
Saturated fat **1g.**
Sodium **315mg.**

2 lb. mussels, scrubbed and debearded
2 large shallots, finely chopped
2 garlic cloves, finely chopped
1 bay leaf
⅛ tsp. dried thyme leaves
25 black peppercorns (about ½ tsp.), placed in a small plastic bag and crushed with the flat of a knife
½ cup red wine
1 tbsp. red wine vinegar
1 tbsp. olive oil

Place 1 pound of the mussels, the shallots, garlic, bay leaf, thyme, peppercorns and wine in a deep dish. Cover the dish and microwave it on high for two minutes. Set aside the mussels that have opened. If there are any that remain tightly closed, re-cover the dish and microwave it on high for 30 seconds more. Again set aside the mussels that have opened. Microwave any remaining unopened mussels on high for 30 seconds; set the opened ones aside and discard any that stay closed. Add the remaining pound of mussels to the dish and cook them the same way.

When all of the mussels have been cooked, pour the vinegar and oil into the dish, cover it, and microwave the mixture on high for two minutes. Return the mussels to the dish, stirring to coat them with the liquid, and cover the dish once more. Microwave on high for one minute to heat the mussels through. Serve the mussels in their shells directly from the dish, or transfer them to a serving bowl along with their sauce.

Crab Meat with Tomatoes, Mushrooms and Garlic

Serves 4
Working (and total) time: about 25 minutes

Calories **215**
Protein **22g.**
Cholesterol **86mg.**
Total fat **5g.**
Saturated fat **1g.**
Sodium **245mg.**

1 lb. crab meat, picked over
½ lb. mushrooms, wiped clean and sliced
6 shallots, finely chopped
6 garlic cloves, finely chopped
⅓ cup dry sherry
⅓ cup dry white wine
⅛ tsp. crushed red pepper
1 lb. ripe tomatoes, peeled, seeded and chopped
2 tbsp. chopped fresh parsley
1 tbsp. virgin olive oil

Combine the mushrooms, shallots, garlic, sherry, wine and crushed red pepper in a baking dish. Cover the dish tightly and microwave it on high for eight minutes, stirring once midway through the cooking time.

Add the crab meat, tomatoes, parsley and oil, and toss well. Cover the dish tightly, microwave on high for two minutes and serve immediately. (If you prefer, spoon individual portions into ceramic or natural crab shells before serving.)

SUGGESTED ACCOMPANIMENT: *escarole salad.*

Oysters and Pasta Shells in Mornay Sauce

Serves 4
Working (and total) time: about 20 minutes

Calories **335**
Protein **21g.**
Cholesterol **88mg.**
Total fat **12g.**
Saturated fat **4g.**
Sodium **315mg.**

1 pint shucked oysters, drained
¼ lb. medium pasta shells
1 tbsp. safflower oil
1 tbsp. finely chopped shallot
2 oz. Gruyère cheese, coarsely grated (about ½ cup)
2 tbsp. flour
1 cup low-fat milk
grated nutmeg
⅛ tsp. salt
white pepper
1 tbsp. fresh bread crumbs
½ tsp. paprika

Cook the pasta in 1 quart of boiling water with ¼ tea-spoon of salt; start testing the shells after 10 minutes and cook them until they are *al dente*. Drain the shells, put them in a bowl and cover them with cold water.

Place the oil and shallot in another bowl, cover the bowl with plastic wrap or a lid, and microwave it on high for 45 seconds. Toss the cheese with the flour, evenly coating the cheese, and add this mixture to the bowl. Pour in the milk, then stir in a pinch of nutmeg, the salt and some white pepper. Cover the bowl again and microwave it on high for three minutes. Remove the bowl from the oven and stir the sauce.

Drain the reserved pasta and combine it with the sauce. Gently stir in the oysters, then transfer the mixture to a shallow baking dish. Cover the dish and microwave it on medium (50 percent power) for five minutes. Remove the dish from the oven and stir to blend the oyster liquid into the sauce. Combine the bread crumbs with the paprika and sprinkle them over the top. Serve immediately.

SUGGESTED ACCOMPANIMENT: *sautéed red peppers.*

Lobster with Chanterelles and Madeira

Serves 2
Working time: about 20 minutes
Total time: about 30 minutes

Calories **315**
Protein **30g.**
Cholesterol **120mg.**
Total fat **8g.**
Saturated fat **4g.**
Sodium **420mg.**

2 live lobsters (about 1¼ lb. each)
½ cup Madeira
1 tbsp. unsalted butter
1 shallot, finely chopped
¼ lb. chanterelles
1 tsp. cornstarch, mixed with 1½ tsp. water
1 small tomato, peeled, seeded and cut into thin strips

To kill the lobsters without cooking the meat, drop them into a large pot of boiling water. Tightly cover the pot and boil the lobsters for one minute. Remove the lobsters with tongs and let them drain.

To ensure that the lobsters cook evenly in the micro- wave oven, thread a wooden skewer through each lobster's tail until the skewer pierces the body. Position the lobsters with their heads pointing in opposite di- rections in a shallow dish. Pour in the Madeira, cover the dish with plastic wrap, and microwave it on high for four to five minutes. Turn the dish a half turn and cook again until the lobsters turn red — four to five minutes more. Remove the meat from the lobsters as demonstrated on pages 134 and 135.

Put the butter in a bowl and microwave it on high for 40 seconds. Gently stir in the shallot and chanterelles, coating them with the butter, and microwave the mix- ture on high for two minutes more.

Transfer the lobster meat to a serving platter. Pour the liquid remaining in the dish into the bowl contain- ing the chanterelles. Gently stir in the cornstarch mix- ture and the tomato strips. Partially cover the bowl and microwave it on high for three minutes. Stir the sauce, then pour it around the lobster meat on the platter.

SUGGESTED ACCOMPANIMENT: *linguine.*

Roulades of Flounder with Seaweed, Spinach and Rice

Serves 4
Working time: about 20 minutes
Total time: about 45 minutes

Calories **245**
Protein **25g.**
Cholesterol **55mg.**
Total fat **2g.**
Saturated fat **1g.**
Sodium **665mg.**

1 lb. flounder or sole fillets, cut lengthwise into 8 equal pieces
½ cup white rice
1¼ cups unsalted tomato juice
½ tsp. fennel seeds
¼ tsp. salt
½ lb. fresh spinach
white pepper
2 sheets nori (dried roasted seaweed)
1 tbsp. cornstarch
1 cup fish stock (recipe, page 136)
2 tbsp. mirin (sweetened Japanese rice wine) or cream sherry
2 tbsp. low-sodium soy sauce
2 tsp. rice vinegar
4 or 5 drops hot red-pepper sauce
2 tbsp. chopped fresh parsley

To prepare the filling, combine the rice, tomato juice, fennel seeds and salt in a 1-quart measuring cup or glass bowl and cover it. Microwave the filling on high for 12 minutes, then set it aside, still covered.

Wash and stem the spinach. Put the spinach with just the water that clings to it into a 2-quart baking dish. Cover the dish with heavy-duty plastic wrap and microwave it on high for three minutes. Remove the spinach from the oven and let it cool.

Rinse the fillets under cold running water and pat them dry with paper towels. Lay the fillets side by side, with their darker sides up, on a work surface; season them with the white pepper. Spread a thin layer of the rice filling on each fillet. Cut a strip of *nori* to fit each fillet. Lay the strips in place atop the rice, then cover each strip of *nori* with some spinach. Roll each fillet into a roulade, rolling end to end as you would do to form a jelly roll.

Mix the cornstarch with two tablespoons of the stock; then, in the same dish you used to cook the spinach, stir together the remaining stock, the cornstarch mixture, the mirin, soy sauce, vinegar and hot sauce. Microwave the mixture on high for three minutes; stir the resulting sauce until it is smooth. Lay the roulades in the sauce, their seam sides down; they should be close but not touching. Cover the dish and microwave it on high for six minutes. Let the dish stand for three minutes. Just before serving the roulades, spoon some of the sauce over them and garnish them with the parsley.

SUGGESTED ACCOMPANIMENT: *red cabbage salad.*

Haddock with Chicory and Bacon

Serves 4
Working (and total) time: about 20 minutes

Calories **150**	*1 lb. haddock fillets (or cod, pollock or scrod)*
Protein **24g.**	*2 garlic cloves, finely chopped*
Cholesterol **69mg.**	*2 tbsp. fresh lemon juice*
Total fat **3g.**	*1 tsp. fresh rosemary, or ¼ tsp. dried rosemary, crumbled*
Saturated fat **1g.**	*freshly ground black pepper*
Sodium **270mg.**	*2 strips of bacon*
	1 head of chicory (about 1 lb.), trimmed, washed and cut into 1-inch pieces
	⅛ tsp. salt

Rinse the haddock under cold running water and pat it dry with paper towels. Cut it into four serving pieces. Rub the fish with half of the garlic, 1 tablespoon of the lemon juice, the rosemary and a generous grinding of pepper. Set the fish aside.

Cut the bacon strips crosswise in two and put them in the bottom of a large dish. Microwave the bacon on high until it is done but not crisp — about two minutes. Lay a strip of bacon on top of each piece of fish.

Add the remaining garlic to the bacon fat in the dish. Add the chicory to the dish along with the remaining tablespoon of lemon juice, the salt and some pepper. Toss the chicory to distribute the seasonings, then mound it in the center of the dish. Microwave the dish on high for two minutes. Briefly toss the chicory again and then microwave it on high until it wilts — about two minutes more.

Lay the fish on top of the chicory. Microwave the fish on medium (50 percent power) until the flesh is opaque — five to six minutes. Remove the dish from the oven and spoon the juices that have collected in the bottom into a small saucepan. Boil the juices rapidly until only 2 tablespoons of liquid remain; pour the sauce over the fish and serve at once.

SUGGESTED ACCOMPANIMENT: *curried rice.*

Swordfish Steaks with Lemon, Orange and Lime

Serves 4
Working time: about 15 minutes
Total time: about 35 minutes

Calories **250**		
Protein **30g.**	1½ lb. swordfish steak (or shark or tuna), trimmed and cut into quarters	
Cholesterol **73mg.**	1 lemon	
Total fat **12g.**	1 orange	
Saturated fat **3g.**	1 lime	
Sodium **155mg.**	1½ tbsp. virgin olive oil	
	1 tsp. fresh rosemary, crushed, or ½ tsp. dried rosemary	
	1 bay leaf, crushed	
	½ tsp. fresh thyme, or ¼ tsp. dried thyme leaves	
	¼ tsp. fennel seeds	
	⅛ tsp. cayenne pepper	

Rinse the swordfish steaks under cold running water and pat them dry with paper towels. Cut the lemon, orange and lime in half. Slice one half of each fruit into wedges and reserve the wedges for garnish. Squeeze the juice from the other halves into a small bowl. Pour the citrus juices over the fish and let the fish marinate at room temperature for 30 minutes.

While the fish is marinating, pour the oil into a 4-ounce ramekin or custard cup. Add the rosemary, bay leaf, thyme, fennel seeds and cayenne pepper. Cover the ramekin with plastic wrap and microwave it on high for two minutes. Set the seasoned oil aside until the fish finishes marinating.

Preheat the microwave browning grill on high for the maximum time allowed in the grill's instruction manual. While the grill is heating, brush the seasoned oil on both sides of each swordfish steak. When the grill is ready, set the steaks on it and cook them on high for 90 seconds. Turn the steaks over and cook them for 90 seconds more — they will still be translucent in the center. Let the steaks stand for a minute, then serve them with the fruit wedges.

SUGGESTED ACCOMPANIMENTS: *bulgur; red-lettuce salad.*
EDITOR'S NOTE: *If you do not have a microwave browning grill, microwave the steaks in an uncovered baking dish for five to six minutes.*

East African Fish Stew

Serves 4
Working time: about 20 minutes
Total time: about 35 minutes

Calories **435**
Protein **22g.**
Cholesterol **22mg.**
Total fat **8g.**
Saturated fat **1g.**
Sodium **185mg.**

½ lb. fresh tuna (or swordfish)
1 tbsp. safflower oil
1 large onion, chopped
2 garlic cloves, finely chopped
1 tsp. ground turmeric
14 oz. canned unsalted whole tomatoes, coarsely chopped, the juice reserved
1 tsp. red wine vinegar
1 tsp. brown sugar
20 saffron threads
⅛ tsp. crushed red pepper
¾ cup rice
¼ tsp. salt
2 boiling potatoes (about ¾ lb.), peeled and cut into ¼-inch cubes
½ cup peas
2 tbsp. fresh lemon juice
2 tbsp. garam masala

In a large glass bowl, stir together the oil, onion, garlic and turmeric. Cover the bowl and microwave it on high until the onions are limp — two to three minutes. Stir in the tomatoes and their juice, the vinegar, brown sugar, saffron threads and red pepper. Cover the bowl and microwave it on high for 10 minutes.

Bring 2 cups of water to a boil in a small saucepan, then add the rice and salt. Cover the pan and cook the rice over medium heat until all the water has been absorbed — about 20 minutes.

While the rice is cooking, finish the stew. Rinse the fish under cold running water, pat it dry with paper towels and cut it into ½-inch cubes. Add the potatoes to the onion-tomato mixture. Cover the bowl and microwave it on high for five minutes. Next add the tuna; cover the bowl and microwave it on high for 10 minutes more, stirring the contents halfway through the cooking time. Finally, add the peas and lemon juice and cook the stew on high, covered, for one minute.

To serve, divide the rice evenly among four bowls. Ladle one fourth of the stew over each serving of rice. Pass the garam masala separately.

EDITOR'S NOTE: *Garam masala, an Indian spice mixture, can be made at home by combining 1 teaspoon each of ground cumin, turmeric, cardamom and coriander with ½ teaspoon each of ground cloves, mace and cayenne pepper and ¼ teaspoon of cinnamon.*

Techniques

Dressing a Roundfish

1 CUTTING OFF THE FINS. Rinse the fish under cold running water, but do not dry it. With a pair of kitchen shears, cut off the fins and discard them. If you intend to cook the fish whole, trim the tail short enough to allow the fish to fit in the cooking vessel.

2 REMOVING THE SCALES. Hold firmly onto the tail with one hand to keep the fish flat on the work surface or in the kitchen sink. Working from the tail to the head, use a fish scaler to scrape off the scales. If you do not have a scaler, a sturdy tablespoon will do.

3 CUTTING OUT THE GILLS. If you plan to cook the fish with the head on, you must remove the gills to avoid a bitter taste. Lift the gill covering on one side, snip around the dark red gill with kitchen shears to remove it. Discard the gill and repeat the procedure for the other gill.

4 SLITTING THE BELLY. Pierce the underside at the anal vent with the tip of a knife and slit the belly toward the head, keeping the cut shallow enough to avoid cutting into the viscera. Alternatively, cut open with kitchen shears. (If the head is to be removed, slit the belly from front to vent.)

5 GUTTING. *Reach into the belly with your fingers and pull out the viscera. Use a knife or scissors to sever and remove any visceral attachments; then break the membrane lining the belly on either side of the backbone to release any accumulated blood. Thoroughly rinse out the belly cavity and gill area.*

6 SEVERING THE HEAD. *With a large chef's knife or a cleaver, cut off the head at an angle just behind the gill openings. If the backbone is especially hard, turn the fish on its belly and cut into the neck behind the gills to sever the backbone. Then remove the head as indicated above. If you wish, use the head for stock.*

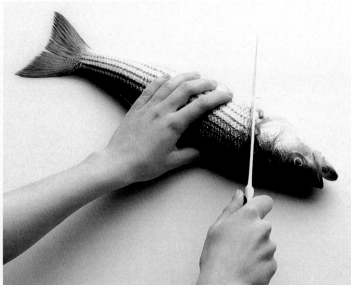

Skinning a Catfish or an Eel

1 PIERCING THE SKIN. *Gut the catfish and rinse it well. Grip the head with a towel to protect your hand from the barbed fins. Using a sharp knife, cut all around the head, angling the cut to fall behind the pectoral fins. Make another cut along the back, as shown. (Cut an eel around the neck.)*

2 STRIPPING AWAY THE SKIN. *Loosen a flap of skin behind the head. Holding the fish down, grasp the flap with pliers and pull the skin from one side of the body. Repeat the procedure on the other side. (An eel's skin should come off in a tubular sheath.) To fillet the catfish, see the instructions on page 130.*

Filleting a Roundfish

1 *CUTTING BEHIND THE HEAD. Snip off the fins, and scale and gut the fish. Rinse it thoroughly under cold running water, making sure the abdominal cavity is clean. Place a filleting or flexible boning knife at a diagonal behind the head of the fish and cut down to the backbone without severing it.*

2 *CUTTING ALONG THE BACKBONE. Position the fish on the work surface with the tail pointing toward you. Hold the fish steady on the work surface and place the knife just above the bony ridge of the spine. Cut along the length of the backbone, from the neck to the tail, about ½ inch deep.*

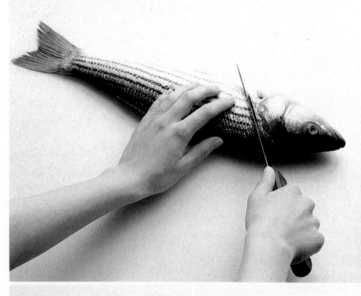

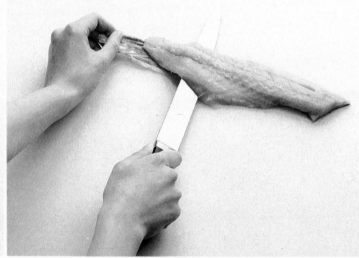

3 *REMOVING THE FILLETS. Insert the knife into the cut and trim the flesh from the rib cage with short strokes, cutting parallel to the bones. Peel back the flesh with your other hand as you go, until the fillet comes away in a strip. Flip the fish over, turn the head toward you, and repeat the procedure.*

4 *SKINNING THE FILLETS. Place a fillet skin side down on the work surface. Trim a small piece of flesh from the tail end. Holding onto the exposed skin, place a knife (here, a slicer) between the flesh and the skin. With the blade angled slightly downward, run the knife along the skin to separate the fillet.*

Filleting a Flatfish

1 *CUTTING BEHIND THE HEAD. Rinse the fish under cold running water, but do not dry it. With a filleting or flexible boning knife, make a V-shaped cut behind the head, slicing down to the backbone without severing it. Around the belly, cut through the flesh, taking care not to pierce the viscera.*

2 *CUTTING DOWN THE BACKBONE. Position the fish on the work surface with the tail pointing toward you. Place the knife at the point of the "V" and make a straight cut down the center line of the fish from the neck to the tail, following the ridge of the backbone.*

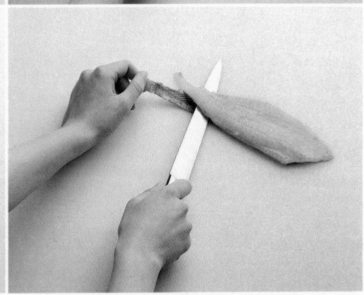

3 *REMOVING THE FILLETS. Insert the knife into the cut and trim a fillet from the rib cage with short strokes, cutting parallel to the bones. Peel back the flesh as you go, until the fillet comes away in a strip. Rotate the fish to fillet the other side. Then flip the fish over and repeat the procedures.*

4 *SKINNING THE FILLETS. Place a fillet skin side down on the work surface. Trim a small piece of flesh from the tail end. Holding onto the exposed skin with your fingers, place a knife (here, a slicer) between the flesh and the skin. With the blade angled slightly downward, run the knife along the skin to separate the fillet.*

Preparing a Squid for Cooking

1 *SEPARATING THE POUCH AND TENTACLES. Working over a bowl of water or a sink, hold the squid's pouch in one hand and its tentacles in the other. Gently pull the tentacles until the viscera separate from the inside of the pouch. Set the tentacles aside, with the head and viscera still attached.*

2 *REMOVING THE PEN. Feel inside the pouch with your fingers to locate the pen, or quill — a cartilaginous structure running nearly the length of the pouch. Pull out the pen and discard it. Reach inside the pouch and scrape out any remaining gelatinous material with your fingers; wash the pouch thoroughly.*

3 *SKINNING THE POUCH. Starting at the open end of the pouch, use your fingers to pull the mottled purplish skin away from the pale flesh. Continue peeling off the skin from the pouch; discard the skin. Rinse the pouch again, then set it aside in a bowl of fresh cold water.*

4 *CUTTING OFF THE TENTACLES. Lay the viscera, head and tentacles on a cutting board. Sever the tentacles from the head below the eyes; the tentacles should remain joined togehter by a narrow band of flesh. Discard the head and viscera. If any of the bony beak remains in the tentacle section, squeeze it out.*

Preparing Crabs

1 *REMOVING THE APRON. If the live crabs are sandy, wash them under cold water, using tongs to protect yourself from the pincers. After cooking the crabs, locate the apron, or tail flap, on each crab's underside. With a fingertip or the point of a small knife, pry the flap up and bend it back until it snaps off.*

2 *SEPARATING THE TOP SHELL. With the crab turned upside down, place your thumbs on either side of the gap left by the apron and gently pry the top shell away from the body. Sometimes the viscera will come off with the shell. If they do, discard the viscera and the shell.*

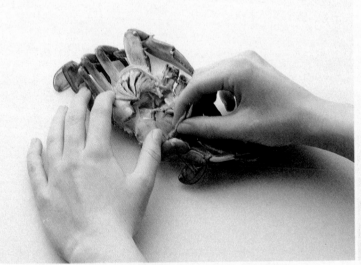

3 *REMOVING THE GILLS. Pluck out the inedible, spongy gills. Twist off the appendages that protrude from the crab's mouth end. Remove the viscera from the middle of the crab, if they did not come away with the shell. Discard the gills, appendages and viscera.*

4 *DIVIDING THE BODY. Bend the crab's body back and forth until it snaps in two. Twist off the claws and legs. Remove the backfin, or lump, meat with your fingers or a small fork. Crack the claws with a nutcracker or a crab mallet and remove the meat. Break the legs at the joints and extract the meat with a pick.*

Preparing a Lobster

1 *SEPARATING THE TAIL FROM THE BODY. Place a cooked lobster right side up on a work surface. Hold the thorax, or body, portion firmly with one hand, and with the other hand twist the tail section, pulling it free of the body.*

2 *EXTRACTING THE TAIL MEAT. Holding the tail section upside down in the palm of one hand, snip down both sides of the thin shell with kitchen shears. Be careful not to cut into the meat beneath. Lift the meat from the tail in one piece and set it aside.*

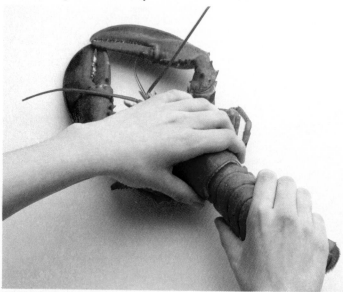

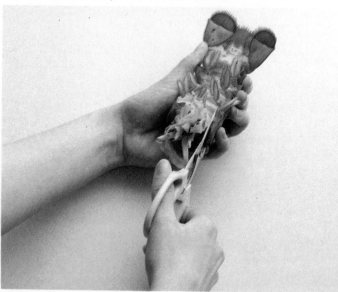

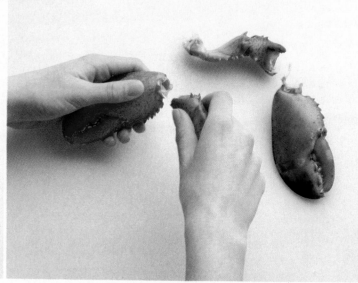

3 *REMOVING THE CLAWS AND LEGS. With your fingers, grasp a claw near its base and twist it off. Twist off the other claw and the eight small legs. Break each leg apart at the central joint; then, with a small pick or a skewer, remove the slivers of flesh inside.*

4 *SEPARATING THE CLAW AT THE JOINT. Holding the claw by the pincer in one hand, firmly grasp the first joint with the other hand and twist it to free it from the pincer. Repeat the procedure to separate the other claw at its joint.*

5 CRACKING THE CLAWS. With a nutcracker or a pair of slip-joint pliers held at a slight diagonal to the claw's widest point, crack a claw. Lift away any shell fragments and carefully pull out the claw meat. Crack the joint segments and remove the meat. Repeat the procedure with the other claw.

6 SPLITTING THE BODY. Place the body on its back and split it down the center with a large knife. Discard the viscera and the sand sac found near the head. Scrape out the edible greenish tomalley, or liver, and the reddish orange roe, if it is present. Use a pick or fork to extract any meaty tidbits from the body.

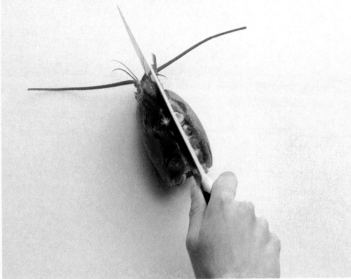

Shucking an Oyster

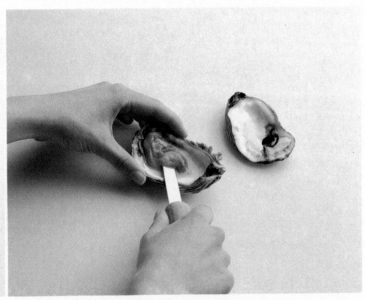

1 OPENING THE SHELLS. Scrub the oyster well. Place it on a work surface with its rounder side down to catch the liquid. Grip the oyster with a towel to protect your hand, leaving the hinged end exposed, and force the tip of an oyster knife into the hinge. Twist the blade to pry the shells apart.

2 FREEING THE OYSTER. Sliding the knife blade along the inside of the upper shell, sever the muscle that attaches the flesh to the shell. Discard the upper shell, then slide the blade under the oyster and cut it free. Save the rounder shells, if you like, and use them to serve the oysters in.

Court Bouillon

Makes about 3 quarts
Working time: about 10 minutes
Total time: about 35 minutes

4 onions, thinly sliced
3 celery stalks, thinly sliced
2 carrots, peeled and thinly sliced
½ cup loosely packed parsley stems
3 fresh thyme sprigs, or 1 tsp. dried thyme leaves
4 garlic cloves, crushed
2 bay leaves, crumbled
1 tsp. anise or fennel seeds (optional)
1½ cups dry white wine
¼ cup white wine vinegar
5 whole peppercorns, cracked

Put the onions, celery, carrots, parsley, thyme, garlic, bay leaves, and anise or fennel seeds, if you are using them, into a large, nonreactive stockpot. Pour in 3 quarts of water, cover the pot, and bring the liquid to a boil. Reduce the heat and simmer the liquid, with the lid slightly ajar, for 15 minutes.

Add the wine, vinegar and peppercorns, and simmer the court bouillon for 15 minutes more. Strain the liquid through a fine sieve into a bowl or a clean pan before using it.

Fish Stock

Makes about 2 quarts
Working time: about 15 minutes
Total time: about 40 minutes

2 lb. lean-fish bones, fins and tails discarded, the bones rinsed thoroughly and chopped into large pieces
2 onions, thinly sliced
2 celery stalks, chopped
1 carrot, peeled and thinly sliced
2 cups dry white wine
2 tbsp. fresh lemon juice
1 leek (optional), trimmed, split, washed thoroughly to remove all grit, and sliced
3 garlic cloves (optional), crushed
10 parsley stems
3 fresh thyme sprigs, or 1 tsp. dried thyme leaves
1 bay leaf, crumbled
5 black peppercorns, cracked

Put the fish bones, onions, celery, carrot, wine, lemon juice, 2 quarts of water, and the leek and garlic, if you are using them, in a large nonreactive stockpot. Bring the liquid to a boil, then reduce the heat to medium to maintain a strong simmer. Skim off all the scum that rises to the surface.

Add the parsley, thyme, bay leaf and peppercorns. Reduce the heat to medium low and simmer the stock for 20 minutes.

Strain the stock through a fine sieve lined with cheesecloth. Allow the stock to cool before refrigerating or freezing it.

EDITOR'S NOTE: *The stock will keep for three days in the refrigerator. Stored in small, well-sealed freezer containers, the stock may be kept frozen for as long as two months.*

Because the bones from oilier fish produce a strong flavor, be sure to use only the bones from lean fish. Sole, flounder, turbot and other flatfish are best.

Glossary

Anise seeds: the licorice-flavored seeds of a plant native to the Middle East. It is used in certain curries and to flavor sauces.

Anisette: a clear, sweet liqueur made from herbs and seeds, among them anise seeds.

Apron: the triangular or T-shaped flap found on the underside of a crab's shell. The apron varies in size or shape depending on the species. The female blue crab's apron is broad and triangular, the male's thin and elongated.

Balsamic vinegar: a mild, dark red, intensely fragrant wine-based vinegar made in Modena, Italy; traditionally aged in wooden casks.

Bamboo shoots: the cream-colored, crisp young shoots of the bamboo plant. Raw bamboo shoots are poisonous; they must be cooked before eating.

Basil: a leafy herb in the mint family, with a strong, pungent aroma when fresh. If they are covered with olive oil and refrigerated in a tightly sealed container, whole fresh basil leaves may be kept for several months.

Bass, black sea: a gray to blue-black Atlantic fish that weighs from one to five pounds. It has lean, mild-flavored, firm flesh.

Bass, striped (also called rockfish in the Chesapeake Bay region): a migratory fish with seven or eight stripes on its silver sides. It has been successfully transplanted to the Pacific Ocean from the Atlantic. The market size of striped bass ranges from three to 10 pounds; the flesh is lean, white and moist. Peak availability is in the fall.

Bass, white sea: the name applied to a large drum found off the California coast. Its weight ranges from 10 to 50 pounds; the flesh is lean and firm. A popular sport fish, white sea bass is available fresh during the summer.

Bay leaves: the pungent dried leaves of the bay or laurel tree *(Laurus nobilis)*, a Mediterranean evergreen, or of the stronger-flavored California bay tree. Many cooks prefer Mediterranean bay leaves for their more subtle taste.

Belgian endive: a small, cylindrical vegetable, composed of many tightly wrapped white to pale yellow leaves. It has the characteristic astringent flavor of all endive.

Black sea bass: see Bass, black sea.

Black vinegar, Chinese (also called Chenkong vinegar, Chinkiang vinegar): a dark vinegar made from fermented rice. Balsamic vinegar may be used as a substitute.

Blanch: to partially cook food by briefly immersing it in boiling water. Blanching makes such thin-skinned vegetables as tomatoes easier to peel; it can also mellow strong flavors.

Blue crab: a species of crab with a blue-green shell found in bays and channels along the mid- and southern-Atlantic coasts of the United States and in the Gulf of Mexico. It is one of the major domestic species in the United States; the Chesapeake Bay is the largest producer. Its meat is mild and sweet. See also Crab; Soft-shell crab.

Bluefish: a migratory Atlantic fish that appears off the Florida coast in December, swimming north until it reaches New England, where it remains from May until October. The raw flesh is tinged blue, except for a dark, bitter strip that is usually removed. Bluefish can weigh as much as 20 pounds.

Butterfish: a small, bony flatfish that can weigh as little as four ounces. Because of its silvery hue, it is sometimes referred to as dollarfish. It is called Pacific pompano on the West Coast. Its off-white flesh is rich and buttery.

Calorie (or kilocalorie): a unit of heat measurement, used to gauge the amount of energy a food supplies when it is broken down for use in the body.

Caramelize: to heat sugar until the sugar turns brown and syrupy. Also, the process whereby naturally occurring sugars in such foods as shallots and onions change to caramel, contributing a rich flavor.

Cardamom: the bittersweet, aromatic dried seeds of a plant in the ginger family. Cardamom may be used whole or ground.

Carp: a fresh-water fish, ranging from three to 20 pounds, with coarse, rich flesh. The darker flesh is generally cut away and discarded.

Catfish: a scaleless fresh-water fish with tough skin and firm, moist, mild-flavored flesh. Although catfish can weigh as much as 60 pounds, the average market weight is one pound. The skin must be pulled off before cooking *(technique, page 129).*

Cayenne pepper: a fiery powder ground from the seeds and pods of various red chili peppers.

Cherrystone clam: refers to a 2- to 2½-inch quahog or hard clam found on the east coast of the United States. It is usually eaten raw on the half shell. See also Clam; Quahog.

Chicory: a green leafy vegetable with slightly bitter-tasting leaves, often used as a salad green.

Chili paste: a paste of chilies, salt and other ingredients, among them garlic and black beans. Several kinds are available in Asian markets.

Chili peppers: a variety of hot red or green pepper. Serranos and jalapeños are small fresh green chilies that are extremely hot. Anchos are dried poblano chilies that are mildly hot and dark red in color. Fresh or dried, chili peppers contain volatile oils that can irritate the skin and eyes; they must be handled with extreme care *(caution, page 41).*

Chinese black vinegar: see Black vinegar, Chinese.

Chinese parsley: see Cilantro.

Cholesterol: a waxlike substance that is manufactured in the liver and also derived from foods of animal origin only. Although a certain amount of cholesterol is necessary for producing hormones and building cell walls, an excess can accumulate in the arteries, contributing to heart disease. See also Monounsaturated fats; Polyunsaturated fats; Saturated fats.

Chutney: an Indian relish that can be made of fruits, vegetables, spices, vinegar and sugar. It is served cooked or raw, traditionally with curry. The cooked variety is available bottled.

Cilantro (also called fresh coriander or Chinese parsley): the fresh leaves of the coriander plant; cilantro imparts a lemony, pleasingly pungent flavor to many Latin American, Indian and Asian dishes. Its leaves resemble those of flat-leaved Italian parsley.

Clam: a bivalve mollusk with grayish to whitish shells, found primarily along the Atlantic and Pacific coasts. See also Cherrystone clam; Littleneck clam; Quahog; Razor clam; Soft-shell clam.

Cod: a salt-water fish, normally weighing between six and 15 pounds, that is caught year round in the Atlantic and Pacific Oceans. Its lean, white flesh flakes easily when cooked. A cod weighing less than two pounds may be called scrod. See also Haddock; Hake; Pollock; Scrod.

Coriander: an herb whose earthy-tasting seeds are often used as an ingredient in curries. See also Cilantro.

Court bouillon: a flavored liquid used for poaching fish or shellfish. It may contain aromatic vegetables, herbs, wine or milk.

Couscous: a fine-grained semolina pasta, traditionally served with the classic North African stew of the same name.

Crab: a crustacean with five pairs of jointed legs, the first of which has pincers. It is often sold cooked because of its high perishability. See also Blue crab; Dungeness crab; King crab; Snow crab; Soft-shell crab; Stone crab.

Crayfish (also called crawfish): a fresh-water crustacean similar in appearance to lobster, except that it is much smaller — its body measures only from 3½ to 5 inches. Louisiana produces the largest quantity of crayfish in the United States.

Croaker: a member of the drum family, weighing from ½ to three pounds, found in the Atlantic and Pacific Oceans and the Gulf of Mexico, and named for the croaking sound it makes. It has lean and tender flesh. See also Drum.

Cumin: the seeds of a plant related to caraway. They add a pleasantly bitter flavor to curry and chili powders; when toasted, they have a nutty taste.

Daikon radish: a long, white Japanese radish.

Dark sesame oil: a dark seasoning oil, high in polyunsaturated fats, made from toasted sesame seeds. Because the oil has a relatively low smoking point, it is rarely heated. Dark sesame oil should not be confused or replaced with lighter sesame cooking oils.

Debeard: to remove the fibrous threads from a mussel. These tough threads, called the beard, are produced by the mussel to attach itself to stationary objects. See also Mussel.

Devein: to remove the intestinal vein located along the outer curve of a shrimp. Generally done for the sake of appearance. It is easier to remove the vein before cooking the shrimp. To do so, first peel the shrimp; then make a small cut along the line of the vein. Remove the vein manually or rinse the shrimp under cold running water. See also Shrimp.

Dijon mustard: a smooth mustard once manufactured only in Dijon, France; may be flavored with herbs, green peppercorns or white wine.

Drawn: refers to a fish that has had only its scales, gills and viscera removed.

Dressed: refers to a fish that has had its scales, viscera, head, gills and tail removed, and often its fins as well.

Drum: a diverse family of Atlantic and Pacific fish. The name derives from the peculiar sound the fish makes by contracting a muscle against its gas bladder. See also Croaker; Red drum; White sea bass.

Dungeness crab: an especially flavorful species of crab found along the Pacific coast and named after a

Washington town. It is one of the major domestic species. Ranging in size from 1¾ to four pounds, the Dungeness is among the largest of the edible crabs found in North America. See also Crab.

Eel: an Atlantic fish that resembles a snake, with firm, rich flesh and a mild flavor. Eels migrate downriver to the sea to spawn. They are generally skinned before cooking.

Fat: a basic component of many foods, containing three types of fatty acids — saturated, monounsaturated and polyunsaturated — in varying proportions. Fats are usually described as saturated, monounsaturated and polyunsaturated, depending on the mixture of fatty acids they contain. See also Monounsaturated fats; Polyunsaturated fats; Saturated fats.

Fennel (also called Florence fennel or finocchio): a vegetable with feathery green tops and a thick, white, bulbous stalk. It has a milky, licorice flavor and can be eaten raw or cooked. The tops are used both as a garnish and as a flavoring. Fennel is sometimes incorrectly labeled as anise.

Fennel seeds: the aromatic dried seeds of herb fennel, a relative of vegetable fennel; used as a licorice-flavored seasoning in many Italian dishes. It complements seafood and is also an ingredient in curries.

Fermented black beans: soybeans that have been fermented, dried and salted. The beans are often rinsed and crushed before use.

Fillet: a full-length section of a fish cut from the ribs and backbone. Also the act of removing a fillet from a fish (techniques, pages 130 and 131).

Flatfish: flat-bodied fish that swim horizontally along the sea bottom and have both eyes on the same side of the head. Flatfish are easy to fillet and generally are quite lean. See also Flounder; Halibut; Sole; Turbot.

Flounder: a large grouping of flatfish that ranges from the diminutive sand dab to the gigantic halibut. The principal Atlantic varieties include blackback, fluke, gray sole or witch flounder, and yellowtail flounder. West coast varieties include starry flounder, petrale sole, rex sole and sand dab. See also Flatfish; Halibut; Sole; Turbot.

Ginger: the spicy, buff-colored rhizome, or rootlike stem, of the ginger plant, used as a seasoning either in fresh form or dried and powdered. The dried form is not a good substitute for the fresh.

Gratin: a baked dish that has been browned in the oven or under a broiler.

Grouper: a fish caught in temperate and tropical waters around the world. Its flesh is lean, moist and sweet. Depending on the species, groupers range in size from one to 700 pounds. The most important fisheries in the United States are from North Carolina to Florida.

Haddock: a silvery-gray member of the cod family, with lean, delicately flavored flesh. The average weight of haddock is two to five pounds; it is caught in the Atlantic.

Hake (also called whiting): a small member of the cod family, found in the Atlantic, that weighs one to two pounds on average. Hake's lean, mild-flavored flesh is somewhat softer than that of cod.

Halibut: the largest of the flatfish, with lean, moist, firm, white flesh. The Pacific variety can weigh anywhere from 10 to 800 pounds, the rare Atlantic variety as much as 700. Because of its large size, halibut is generally cut up and marketed in steak or fillet form.

Hazelnut: the nut of the hazel shrub or tree. It is rich in oil, with a mild, smoky taste. Hazelnuts are eaten raw or used in sweet cooked dishes.

Herring: a small fish, weighing from ½ to 1½ pounds, dwelling in large schools in the Atlantic and Pacific oceans and the North Sea. The flesh is off-white, rich and soft. Herring is most plentiful at market in the spring.

Hot red-pepper sauce: a hot, unsweetened chili sauce, such as Tabasco.

Italian parsley: a flat-leaved parsley with a more pronounced flavor than curly-leaved parsley.

Jerusalem artichoke (also called sunchoke): neither an artichoke nor from Jerusalem, this American vegetable is the tuberous root of a member of the sunflower family. In texture, color and flavor, it resembles the water chestnut. "Jerusalem" may derive from the Italian word girasole, meaning "a plant whose flowers turn toward the sun."

Julienne: to slice into matchstick-size pieces.

King crab (also called Alaska king crab): a giant species of crab, found on both sides of the North Pacific, that can have a 10-foot span and weigh up to 24 pounds. Only the meat from the claws, legs, shoulders and from below the apron is eaten. Because of overharvesting, king crab is becoming increasingly rare. The meat usually is frozen before shipping. See also Crab.

Leek: a relative of the onion that resembles a large scallion and tastes sweeter and milder than an onion. Must be split and thoroughly washed to rid it of sand and grit.

Littleneck clam: a market name for a 1½-inch quahog or other hard-shell clam found on the east coast of the United States. It is primarily eaten raw on the half shell. The Pacific littleneck clam is a distinct variety and should be cooked. See also Clam; Quahog.

Lobster: a crustacean with a long body and five pairs of jointed legs, the first of which have pincers. The northern lobster, also known as the Maine lobster, is found along the Atlantic coast, from southern Canada to North Carolina. It is characterized by having two large but dissimilar pincers, and is taken when it weighs from one to five pounds. The spiny lobster, actually a sea-dwelling crayfish, is caught off the southeastern coast of the United States and in the Gulf of Mexico. It lacks the large pincers of the northern lobster.

Mace: the covering of the nutmeg seed, ground to a powder for use as a spice.

Mackerel: a rich-fleshed fish, weighing one to four pounds. Atlantic mackerel is striped and ranges from the Gulf of St. Lawrence down to the Carolinas. Spanish mackerel, spotted instead of striped, ranges from the Chesapeake Bay to the South Atlantic. Mackerel's firm flesh, high in oil, flakes easily and lightens in color when cooked. Mackerel is available from fall to spring.

Madeira: a fortified wine, often used in cooking, that is produced on the island of Madeira. There are four classes of Madeira, ranging from sweet to dry in flavor and brown to gold in color.

Mahimahi: the Hawaiian name for dolphinfish, which is caught in semitropical waters of the Pacific and Atlantic oceans. Its size varies from two to 50 pounds; the flesh is lean, firm and flavorful.

Mantle: another name for the body pouch of the squid. It can be sliced or left whole and stuffed.

Marjoram (sweet marjoram and its heartier relative, pot marjoram): an aromatic herb related to, but milder than, oregano.

Marsala: a fortified dessert wine named for the region of Sicily where it originated. Most varieties are sweet in flavor and brown in color.

Mirin: a sweetened Japanese cooking wine made from rice. If mirin is unavailable, substitute white wine or sake mixed with an equal amount of sugar.

Monkfish (also called angler, goosefish and bellyfish): an Atlantic fish with a scaleless, thick-skinned body and an enormous, ugly head; only the tail portion, however, is edible. Although the monkfish weighs on average eight to 15 pounds, some specimens grow as large as 50 pounds. The lean, firm, somewhat dry flesh is thought by some to resemble lobster in flavor.

Monounsaturated fat: one of the three types of fatty acids found in fats. Monounsaturated fats are believed not to raise the level of cholesterol in the blood. Some oils high in monounsaturated fats — olive oil, for example — are thought to lower the blood-cholesterol level.

Mushrooms, dried Asian: Before use, dried Asian mushrooms must be covered with boiling water and soaked for at least 20 minutes, then trimmed of their woody stems. See also Shiitake mushroom.

Mussel: a bivalve mollusk with bluish black shells found along the New England, mid-Atlantic and Pacific coasts. Peak season runs from fall to early spring. The mussel's sweet flesh varies from beige to orange-yellow in color when cooked. See also Debeard.

Nappa cabbage (also called Chinese cabbage): an elongated cabbage resembling romaine lettuce, with long, broad ribs and crinkled, light green to white leaves. Often confused with celery cabbage, which is more elongated and has broader-ribbed leaves.

Nonreactive pan: a cooking vessel whose surface does not react with acids in food. Ovenproof clay, stainless steel, enamel, glass and nonstick-coated aluminum are all considered nonreactive materials.

Nori: paperlike dark green or black sheets of dried seaweed that are often used in Japanese cooking as flavoring or as wrappers for rice and vegetables.

Ocean perch (also called red perch, redfish, rosefish, sea perch): a North Atlantic fish weighing ½ to three pounds. Despite its name, ocean perch does not belong to the perch family; it is a rockfish. Its sweet, rose-colored flesh is lean, firm and moist.

Octopus: a shell-less mollusk of the cephalopod family that inhabits the Atlantic and Pacific. Most of the octopus sold in the markets comes from the Pacific. Octopuses have soft bodies that include an ink sac and, attached to it, eight tentacles covered with suction cups. The usual market size of an octopus is 2½ pounds or less, and most are sold cleaned. The meat is white and mild-flavored and is sometimes served in the ink.

Olive oil: any of various grades of cooking oil extracted from olives. Extra virgin olive oil has a full, fruity flavor and very low acidity. Virgin olive oil is lighter in flavor and slightly higher in acidity. Pure olive oil, a processed blend of olive oils, has the lightest taste and the highest acidity.

Orange roughy: a fish caught commercially off the coast of New Zealand. It has bright orange skin and averages three pounds in weight. The flesh is firm, white and delicate and breaks into large flakes when cooked. It is available, usually marketed in frozen fillets, all year.

Orzo: a rice-shaped dried pasta made of semolina. The word means "barley" in Italian.

Oyster: a bivalve mollusk with two dissimilar shells, found on the Atlantic and Pacific coasts in the shallow waters of bays and estuaries. The size, shape and taste of oysters are determined by the waters in which they grow and the time of year they are harvested. When water temperatures rise, the oysters become more watery in texture, which leads some to say that oysters taste best in cold winter months. Primarily, three species are enjoyed in the United States. The eastern oyster, native to the Atlantic and Gulf coasts, has smooth, thick shells and a mild flavor. Pacific or Japanese oysters grow along the Pacific coast, are large in size and have a strong flavor. Western or Olympia oysters, native to the Northwest, are tiny tender oysters. They are rare in comparison with the other two species.

Papaya: a fruit native to Central America. The color of the skin ranges from green to orange and the flesh from pale yellow to salmon. When ripe, the fruit is sweet and enjoyed raw, but unripe papayas may be eaten cooked as a vegetable.

Paprika: a slightly sweet, brick red powder produced by grinding dried sweet peppers. The best paprika is Hungarian.

Pectoral fins: a pair of fins located behind the gills of a fish.

Pen (also called quill): a piece of cartilage located in the body pouch, or mantle, of a squid. The pen serves as the squid's support structure and should be removed before the squid is cooked. See also Squid.

Penne: a tubular dried semolina pasta with diagonally cut ends. The word means ''pen'' or ''quill'' in Italian.

Phyllo: a Greek pastry dough that is rolled and stretched to tissue-paper thinness. Phyllo is often available frozen.

Pike, Northern: a fresh-water fish commercially available in late spring and summer. The flesh is lean, white and easily flaked.

Plaki: a Greek fish dish baked on a bed of tomatoes.

Poach: to cook something in a barely simmering liquid. Fish is poached in wine, stock or court bouillon. This gentle cooking method keeps food moist and adds flavor to it.

Pollock (also called Boston bluefish): a smaller relative of cod, with a darker tint to the flesh, found in the northern Atlantic and Pacific oceans. The average market weight is four to 12 pounds. The flesh is lean and flakes easily when cooked.

Polyunsaturated fat: one of the three types of fatty acids found in fats. They exist in abundance in such vegetable oils as safflower, corn and soybean. They are also found in seafood. Certain highly polyunsaturated fatty acids called omega-3s occur exclusively in seafood and marine animals. Polyunsaturated fats lower the level of cholesterol in the blood.

Pompano: a silver-colored fish prized for its flavor and texture. It has a high body-fat content. Commercially available pompano, caught primarily in Florida waters, can weigh from ½ to four pounds; the average market weight is 1½ pounds. The flesh is firm, white and buttery.

Porgy (also called scup): a silver, oval-shaped, migratory Atlantic fish. An average porgy weighs one pound, though some specimens may reach five pounds. The lean, sweet flesh has a somewhat coarse texture; the fish itself is quite bony.

Prosciutto: an air-cured ham sliced paper thin. The best is produced near Parma, Italy.

Purge: to cleanse bivalve mollusks of sand and grit. Not absolutely necessary, but done to clams and mussels (method, page 106).

Quahog: a species of hard-shell clam found along the Atlantic coast. The name comes from the Algonquian Indian name for this mollusk, quahaug. Quahogs measuring less than 3 inches in their shells are usually eaten raw; those more than 3 inches long, referred to as chowder clams, are usually cut up and cooked. See also Cherrystone clam; Clam; Littleneck clam.

Quill: see Pen.

Radicchio: a red chicory of Italian origin, with a refreshingly bitter taste. Frequently used in salads.

Ramekin: a small, round, straight-sided glass or porcelain mold, used to bake a single serving of food.

Ray: a boneless fish with a diamond-shaped, flat body adapted to life on the sea bottom. It is similar to the skate but has a long, flexible tail armed near the base with a stinger. See also Skate.

Razor clam: a soft-shell clam found on sandy beaches on the east and west coasts of the United States.

The clams are named for the shape of their long, narrow, sharp shells, which measure about 5 to 7 inches. See also Clam.

Recommended Dietary Allowance (RDA): the average daily amounts of essential nutrients that groups of healthy people of various ages should consume. RDAs are established by the National Research Council.

Red drum (also called channel bass, redfish): a lean fish with fine-textured, sweet flesh. The Atlantic variety usually weighs between 20 and 30 pounds; red drum caught in the Gulf of Mexico normally weigh only four to six pounds. The small red drum, also called puppy drum, is prized for its tenderness. The flesh of large specimens has a slightly coarse texture. See also Drum.

Red snapper: a bright red Atlantic fish weighing between two and six pounds, with red eyes. Not to be confused with Pacific red snapper, which is actually a rockfish.

Reduce: to boil down a liquid in order to concentrate its flavor and thicken its consistency.

Refresh: to rinse a cooked vegetable under cold running water to arrest its cooking and set its color.

Rice vinegar: a mild, fragrant vinegar that is less assertive than cider vinegar or distilled white vinegar. It is available in dark, light, seasoned and sweetened varieties. Japanese rice vinegar generally is milder than the Chinese variety.

Rice wine: Chinese rice wine (shao-hsing) is brewed from rice and wine. Japanese rice wine (sake) has a different flavor, but it may be used as a substitute. If rice wine is unavailable, use sherry in its place. See also Mirin.

Rockfish, Pacific: a fish, often mistakenly called rock cod, that encompasses many varieties, among them yelloweye, canary and bocaccio rockfish. Depending on the depth of the water where they dwell, rockfish can weigh as little as two pounds or as much as 30.

Roe: refers primarily to fish eggs, but edible roe is also found in scallops, crabs and lobsters.

Sablefish (also called black cod): the fattiest of the fish included in this volume, with mild, white, buttery flesh. Sablefish are caught off Alaska and the west coasts of Canada and the United States; they are in greatest supply from summer through fall. They weigh anywhere from three to 40 pounds.

Safflower oil: the vegetable oil that contains the highest proportion of polyunsaturated fats of all the vegetable oils.

Saffron: the dried, yellowish red stigmas (or threads) of the flower of Crocus sativus; saffron yields a pungent flavor and a brilliant yellow color. Although powdered saffron may be substituted for the threads, it is less flavorful.

Salmon, Atlantic: a fish that is supplied chiefly by Canada and Norway. Atlantic salmon weigh between five and 10 pounds; the flesh is light pink and somewhat denser than that of its Pacific cousins.

Salmon, Pacific: a popular fish from the Pacific Northwest. King salmon (or chinook), the fattiest and largest of the salmon, can weigh as much as 30 pounds; the color of its flesh is red. Red (or sockeye) salmon ranges from three to seven pounds, with flesh that is a deep red-orange. Silver (or coho) salmon, weighing between six and 15 pounds, has silvery skin and bright orange flesh. (Farm-raised baby coho is available commercially at 12 ounces.) At an average weight of three to six pounds, pink (or humpback) salmon is the smallest of the Pacific varieties.

Saturated fat: one of the three types of fatty acids present in fats. Found in abundance in animal products and in coconut and palm oils, saturated fats tend to raise the level of blood cholesterol. Because high blood-cholesterol levels contribute to heart disease,

saturated-fat consumption should be kept to a minimum — that is, less than 10 percent of the calories consumed each day.

Sauté: to cook a food quickly in a small amount of butter or oil over high heat, stirring or tossing the food often to keep it from burning or sticking.

Scale: to remove the small, platelike structures covering most fish.

Scallions (also called green onions and spring onions): a slender relative of the onion family, with white bases supporting elongated green leaves.

Scallop: a bivalve mollusk found along the east and west coasts of North America. The round adductor muscle of the animal is the part usually eaten by Americans, although all of the mollusk's meat is edible. Bay, sea and calico scallops are the commercially important species. The bay scallop, found in shallow bays and estuaries along the Atlantic and Gulf coasts, is small — only ½ inch across — and cream or pink in color. Sea scallops are collected in the deep waters of the Atlantic and Pacific oceans and measure up to 2½ inches. Any white connective tissue still attached to sea scallops should be removed before cooking. The calico scallop is found from North Carolina to Florida and in the Gulf of Mexico. It measures ½ to ¾ inches across.

Scrod: a market name that refers to any small northern Atlantic white fish of the cod family. There is no species of fish called scrod.

Sea trout: see Trout, sea.

Sesame oil: see Dark sesame oil.

Seviche (or ceviche): originally a Peruvian dish made of raw white fish or scallops combined with lemon or lime juice, onion, red pepper flakes and black peppercorns. The term is now used to describe any dish in which fish or shellfish is marinated in citrus juice. The acid in the juice breaks down the protein, thus ''cooking'' the raw fish or shellfish.

Shad: a bony Atlantic fish that is a member of the herring family. It has been successfully transplanted to the Pacific. Shad appear off the coast of Florida in December, migrating north until reaching the Gulf of St. Lawrence in May. They swim upriver to spawn; the roe is highly prized.

Shallot: a delicately flavored cousin of the onion, with a papery, red-brown skin.

Shark: a primitive fish without bones or scales found in both the Atlantic and the Pacific oceans. The flesh, similar to that of swordfish, is lean yet full-flavored, firm and dense. Mako shark is preferred for eating.

Shiitake mushroom: a variety of mushroom, originally cultivated only in Japan, sold fresh or dried. See also Mushrooms, dried Asian.

Shrimp: a crustacean that lives in Atlantic and Pacific waters. Although there are hundreds of species, among the most popular are white, brown and pink shrimp. Also eaten in the United States are northern shrimp, caught in the North Atlantic and North Pacific, and rock shrimp, so named because of their tough shells, found primarily around Florida. Virtually all commercially caught shrimp is immediately beheaded and frozen. It is sold in markets according to count per pound; the range is from fewer than 10 per pound to more than 70. Shrimp can be cooked in or out of the shell. Shrimp is moderately high in cholesterol but very low in fat. See also Devein.

Shuck: to remove the meat from the shells of a bivalve mollusk.

Simmer: to cook a liquid or sauce just below its boiling point so that the liquid's surface barely trembles.

Skate: a flat, scaleless, diamond-shaped fish with enlarged pectoral fins called wings; skate is found both in the Atlantic and in the Pacific. The myriad varieties of skate range in weight from two to 100 pounds. The wings provide delicious meat, whose texture and taste — firm and quite sweet — resemble those of scallops. The terms "skate" and "ray" are used interchangeably in markets. See also Ray.

Snow crab: a market name for several varieties of crab, including the snow, tanner and queen species that are found off Canada, Alaska and Maine. The crabs have round bodies and long, smooth, slender legs. The white meat, available cooked, is delicate and can be used interchangeably with other crab meat. See also Crab.

Snow peas: small, flat, green pea pods, eaten whole with only the stems and strings removed. If fresh snow peas are unavailable, substitute green peas or broccoli stems; frozen snow peas are soggy by comparison.

Sodium: a nutrient essential to maintaining the proper balance of fluids in the body. In most diets, a major source of the element is table salt, made up of 40 percent sodium. Excess sodium may contribute to high blood pressure, which increases the risk of heart disease. One teaspoon of salt — with about two grams, or 2,100 milligrams, of sodium — contains about two thirds of the maximum "safe and adequate" daily sodium intake recommended by the National Research Council.

Soft-shell clam: a clam with thin, elongated shells and a long "neck," or siphon, that prevents the clam from closing completely. Found on both coasts of North America. The most popular way of eating soft-shell clams is steamed, hence their other name — "steamers." Before cooking them, peel away the black "hood" from the neck. See also Clam.

Soft-shell crab: refers to a blue crab that has just molted its hard outer shell. This shedding process occurs as a part of a crab's growth when water temperatures are warm — above 70° F. is best for molting. Most soft-shell crabs are produced in pens or other containers and removed from the water before their new shells begin to harden. Fresh soft-shell crabs are available from late spring to early fall; most are marketed frozen, already cleaned. The entire crab, including its tender shell, is consumed. See also Blue crab; Crab.

Sole: a lean, highly prized fish native to the waters around Great Britain, with firm, white flesh and a delicate flavor. No true sole exists in American waters; local varieties called sole are actually flounder. Certain flounders — notably witch flounder and petrale sole — make suitable substitutions for true sole. See also Flounder.

Soy sauce: a savory, salty, brown liquid made from fermented soybeans. One tablespoon of regular soy sauce contains 1,030 milligrams of sodium; lower-sodium variations may contain as little as half that amount.

Squid: a shell-less mollusk of the cephalopod family found in North American coastal waters. The two main varieties are short-finned and long-finned squid. Eighty percent of the squid — including the tentacles, body pouch, fins and ink — is edible. The pen, beak, ink sac and gonads should be removed before the squid is consumed, if it is bought whole. Squid is high in cholesterol. See also Mantle; Pen.

Steam: to cook food in the vapor from boiling water; steaming is one of the best cooking techniques for preserving nutrients and flavors.

Stir fry: to cook small, uniformly cut vegetables, fish or meat in a short time over high heat in a small amount of oil, stirring constantly to ensure even cooking. The traditional cooking vessel is a wok; a heavy-bottomed skillet can serve instead.

Stock: a savory liquid made by simmering aromatic vegetables, herbs and spices — and bones and trimmings — in water. A vegetarian stock can also be made. Stock forms a flavor-rich base for sauces.

Stone crab: a species of crab named for its hard shell, found in the Gulf and Atlantic waters off Florida. The succulent meat of the black-tipped claws of the crab is the part usually consumed. Stone crabs are shipped frozen or cooked. See also Crab.

Striped bass: see Bass, striped.

Sun-dried tomatoes: Italian plum tomatoes that are air-dried to concentrate their flavor, and sometimes packed in oil. They are now being produced in the United States.

Sweet chili sauce: any of a group of Asian sauces containing chilies, vinegar, sugar and salt. Such a sauce may be used as a condiment to accompany fish, meats or poultry, or it may be included as an ingredient in a dish.

Swordfish: a large fish, weighing between 200 and 500 pounds, found in both the Atlantic and the Pacific. Usually sold in steak form, the flesh is lean, dense and creamy white to pink in color, except for small dark patches.

Tarragon: a strong herb with a sweet anise-like taste. In combination with other herbs — notably sage, rosemary and thyme — it should be used sparingly to avoid a clash of flavors. Because heat intensifies tarragon's flavor, cooked dishes require smaller amounts.

Thyme: a versatile herb with a zesty, slightly fruity flavor and strong aroma.

Tilefish: primarily an Atlantic fish, whose average market weight is six to eight pounds. It has a large head in relation to its body. Although tilefish are multicolored when pulled from the water, the color fades rapidly until only the distinctive yellow spots remain. A Pacific species called ocean whitefish is sometimes found in markets.

Timbale: a creamy mixture of vegetables, meat or fish baked in a mold. The term, French for "drum," also denotes a drum-shaped baking dish.

Tomalley: the greenish liver of a lobster that is savored by itself or used as a flavoring agent.

Tomatillo: a small, tart, green, tomato-like fruit vegetable that is covered with a loose, papery husk. It is frequently used in Mexican dishes.

Total fat: an individual's daily intake of polyunsaturated, monounsaturated and saturated fats. Nutritionists recommend that fat constitute no more than 30 percent of our total energy intake. The term as used in this book refers to all the sources of fats in a recipe.

Trout, lake: a fresh-water fish with firm, fatty flesh; weight can range up to 100 pounds, but the usual size is two to 10 pounds. Lake trout is available in summer.

Trout, rainbow: a fresh-water fish, with an average weight of 1¾ pounds. Most of the commercial supply is farm-raised. The flesh is soft and rich in flavor.

Trout, sea (also called weakfish): a lean Atlantic fish weighing one to five pounds, with fine-textured, mild-flavored flesh.

Tuna: refers to several varieties of fish, found in both the Atlantic and the Pacific; some tuna can weigh as much as 1,500 pounds. The flesh is dense, full-flavored and oily; it can be white, as in albacore tuna, or light brown, as in bigeye and skipjack tuna. Bluefin tuna has dark, nearly red flesh.

Turbot: a flatfish whose high body-fat content (about 10 percent) is unusual for a flatfish. On the east coast of the United States, the most common commercial variety is Greenland turbot. The name "turbot" is also given to certain Pacific flounders. See also Flounder.

Turmeric: a yellow spice from a plant related to ginger, used as a coloring agent and occasionally as a substitute for saffron. Turmeric has a musty odor and a slightly bitter flavor.

Virgin olive oil: see Olive oil.

Walleye: widely described as a pike; it is actually the largest of the fresh-water perch. The lean, white, flaky flesh is highly prized for its sweetness.

Wasabi: a Japanese horseradish, usually sold in powdered form. The powder is mixed with water to form a fiery green paste, which is then served with sushi or noodles.

Water chestnut: the walnut-size tuber of an aquatic Asian plant, with rough brown skin and white, sweet, crisp flesh. Fresh water chestnuts may be refrigerated for up to two weeks; they must be peeled before use. A crisp, mild vegetable such as jícama or Jerusalem artichoke makes an acceptable substitute.

Weakfish: see Trout, sea.

White pepper: a powder ground from the same berry as that used to produce black pepper. For white pepper, the berries are allowed to ripen on the vine longer and are ground without their shells, resulting in a milder flavor.

White sea bass: see Bass, white sea.

Whitefish (also called lake whitefish): a fish of the salmon and trout family, weighing from one to five pounds, caught in lakes in the north central United States and in Canada. The flesh is white, rich and tender, breaking easily into large flakes after cooking.

Whiting: see Hake.

Wild rice: the seed of a water grass native to the Great Lakes region of the United States. It is appreciated for its nutty flavor and chewy texture.

Yogurt: a smooth-textured, semisolid cultured milk product made with varying percentages of fat. Yogurt makes an excellent substitute for sour cream in cooking. Yogurt also may be combined with sour cream to produce a sauce or topping that is lower in fat and calories than sour cream alone.

Zest: the flavorful outermost layer of citrus-fruit rind, cut or grated free of the bitter white pith that lies beneath it.

Index

Picture Credits

All of the photographs in *Fresh Ways with Fish and Shellfish* were taken by staff photographer Renée Comet unless otherwise indicated:

2: top and center, Carolyn Wall Rothery. 4: lower right, Michael Latil. 5: lower left, Michael Latil. 6: John D. Dawson. 27: top, Michael Latil. 31: Steven Biver. 33: Aldo Tutino. 39: Steven Biver. 41: Aldo Tutino. 46: Steven Biver. 47: Michael Latil. 48: bottom, Michael Latil. 54: Michael Latil. 60: top, Michael Latil. 72: Michael Latil. 77, 78: Michael Latil. 80, 81: Michael Latil. 86: left, Michael Latil. 90-92: Michael Latil. 93: top, Michael Latil. 94-99: Michael Latil. 101, 102: Michael Latil. 104, 105: Michael Latil. 108: Michael Latil. 111: left, Michael Latil; right, Taran Z. 119, 120: Michael Latil. 124-126: Michael Latil. 128-135: Taran Z.

Props: cover: Cambet de France, Washington, D.C. 12: Cliff Lee, Lee Gallery, Washington, D.C. 13: Cliff Lee, Lee Gallery. 15: Gear Stores, New York, N.Y. 18: server, Retroneu, New York, N.Y. 19: picnic set and fabric, Carol Overdorf Antiques, Washington, D.C. 20: Mary George Kronstadt, Washington, D.C. 22: platter, Bowl & Board, Washington, D.C.; fabric, Blue Moon, Washington, D.C. 23: plate and flatware, Martin's of Georgetown, Washington, D.C.; inset, background, Joyce Piotrowski. 24: platter and plate, Barbara Eigen, New York, N.Y.; rug, Buffalo Gallery, Alexandria, Va.; wood, Austin Hardwoods Co., Lorton, Va.; pitcher, Mary Jane Blandford. 26: Bruce Gholson, The American Hand Plus, Washington, D.C.

27: Susquehanna Antique Co., Inc., Washington, D.C. 29: Ellen Godwin. 30: steamer basket, Sharon Farrington. 34: plates and flatware, Martin's of Georgetown. 35: Ann Elizabeth Design, Williamstown, Mass. 37: pewter, Susquehanna Antique Co., Inc.; fabric, Joyce Piotrowski. 38: Joyce Piotrowski; flower container, Paulette Comet. 42: Royal Worcester Spode Inc., New York, N.Y. 43: Mary George Kronstadt. 46: Vietri platter, Jane Wilner, Washington, D.C. 47: Micheline's Country French Antiques, Alexandria, Va. 48: bowl, China Closet, Bethesda, Md.; tile, Country Floors, Inc., New York, N.Y. 49: Uzzolo, Washington, D.C. 50: Cherishables Antiques, Washington, D.C. 51: plate, Martin's of Georgetown; background, plate, Elayne De Vito. 52: Gear Stores. 53: WILTON Armetale, New York, N.Y. 54: plate and placemat, Jane Wilner; fork, Cambet de France. 57: Joyce Piotrowski. 59: platter, Gertrude Berman; fish service, Joan Burka. 60: Scandinavian Galleries, Washington, D.C. 62: platter and plates, Louise Harts Antiques, Alexandria, Va.; bowls, Nelson-French Antiques, Inc., Washington, D.C.; fish service, Joan Burka; tablecloth, Sylvia Heitner. 64: Mary George Kronstadt. 65: platter, Deruta of Italy, Corp., New York, N.Y.; servers, Retroneu; fish, Gossypia, Alexandria, Va. 66: flies and case, Tom Suzuki. 69: Lenox China, James Kaplan Jewelers, Cranston, R.I. 70-71: net, Shepherd's Live Bait & Tackle, Alexandria, Va.; oyster pail, Chesapeake Bay Maritime Museum, St. Michaels, Md. 73: Skellin and Company, Bethesda, Md. 75: Sharon Farrington. 76: Richard Meier for Swid Powell, The American Hand Plus. 77: Mariposa, New York, N.Y. 78: Mark Anderson, Torpedo Factory Art Center, Alexandria, Va. 79: Mikasa,

New York, N.Y. 81: Geff Reed, The American Hand Plus. 84: Royal Worcester Spode Inc.; fork, Wilfred-Rodgers, Alexandria, Va. 85: Country Floors, Inc. 86-87: 219 Restaurant, Alexandria, Va. 89: plate, The Pilgrim Glass Corp., New York, N.Y.; oyster pail and culling hammer, Chesapeake Bay Maritime Museum. 91: Stanley Anderson, The American Hand Plus. 94-95: china, Mikasa Factory Outlet, Reading, Pa.; flatware, Martin's of Georgetown; candlestick, Marc Westen Decorative Arts, Washington, D.C.; flowers and vase, Flowers Unique, Inc., Alexandria, Va; tablecloth and napkins, Gertrude Berman. 96: plate, Micheline's Country French Antiques; tablecloth, Gertrude Berman. 98: Rose Lee, Potters' Studio, Berkeley, Calif. 99: bowl, Nelson-French Antiques, Inc.; flatware, Retroneu; fabric, Skellin and Company. 100: Beth Armour, Putney, Vt.; baskets, Joyce Piotrowski. 102: bowl, Fil Caravan Inc., New York, N.Y.; fabric, Carol Overdorf Antiques. 103: plate, The Pilgrim Glass Corp.; basket, Skellin and Company. 105: Skellin and Company. 106: plates, Royal Worcester Spode Inc.; fork, Joan Burka. 107: James II Galleries, New York, N.Y. 108: bowls, WILTON Armetale; server, Retroneu. 109: platter, Ginza "Things Japanese," Washington, D.C. 110: Evelyn Kielty Unger, Burnville, N.C. 112: bowl and plate, Geff Reed, The American Hand Plus; fabric, Louis Lochary. 115: left, Skellin and Company. 116: Country Floors, Inc. 117: Susan Greenleaf, Fire One, Torpedo Factory Art Center. 118: Luna Garcia, Venice, Calif. 120: Rob Barnard, Anton Gallery, Washington, D.C. 121: left, platter, Bowl & Board. 122: Joyce Piotrowski. 123: tablecloth, Sylvia Heitner. 124: plate, Mark Anderson, Torpedo Factory Art Center; servers, Retroneu.

Acknowledgments

The index for this book was prepared by Barbara Klein. The editors are particularly indebted to the following people for creating recipes for this volume: Nora Carey, Paris, France; Robert Carmack, Camas, Wash.; Sharon Farrington, Bethesda, Md.; Faye Levy, Santa Monica, Calif.

The editors also wish to thank: Alaska Fisheries Development Foundation, Anchorage, Alaska; Alaska Seafood Marketing Institute, Juneau, Alaska; The Amber Grain, Washington, D.C.; Jim Barklow, Jake's Famous Crawfish and Seafoods, Inc., Portland, Ore.; Martha Blacksall, BBH Corporation, Washington, D.C.; Jo Calabrese, Royal Worcester Spode Inc., New York, N.Y.; Jackie Chalkley, Washington, D.C.; Chicago Fish House, Chicago, Ill.; Nic Colling, Home Produce Company, Alexandria, Va.; Gene Cope, Lou Kissel, National Marine Fisheries Service, Department of Commerce, Washington, D.C.; Jeanne Dale, The Pilgrim Glass Corp., New York, N.Y.; Paul Dexter, Salvatore Termini, Deruta of

Italy Corp., New York, N.Y.; Rex Downey, Oxon Hill, Md.; Dr. Jacob Exler, U.S. Department of Agriculture, Hyattsville, Md.; Nancy Fennel, Oregon Dungeness Crab Commission, Salem, Ore.; Dr. George Flick, Virginia Polytechnic Institute, Blacksburg, Va.; Flowers Unique, Inc., Alexandria, Va.; Food Marketing Institute, Washington, D.C.; Giant Food, Inc., Landover, Md.; E. Goodwin & Sons, Inc., Jessup, Md.; Great Lakes Fisheries Development Foundation, Grand Haven, Mich.; Gulf and South Atlantic Fisheries Development Foundation, Tampa, Fla.; Chong Su Han, Grass Roots Restaurant, Alexandria, Va.; Wretha Hanson, Franz Bader Gallery, Washington, D.C.; Kathy Hardesty, Columbia, Md.; Steven Himmelfarb, U.S. Fish, Inc., Kensington, Md.; Robert Jordan, Jordan Seafood, Inc., Washington, D.C.; Gary Latzman, Kirk Phillips, Retroneu, New York, N.Y.; Richard Lord, Fulton Market Information Service, New York, N.Y.; Metropolitan Ice and Storage, Washington, D.C.; Mid-Atlantic Fisheries Development Foundation, Inc., Annapolis, Md.; Jorge Mora, Mora Camera Services, Washington,

D.C.; Mutual Fish Company, Inc., Seattle, Wash.; Ed Nash, The American Hand Plus, Washington, D.C.; New England Fisheries Development Foundation, Boston, Mass.; Lisa Ownby, Alexandria, Va.; Joyce Piotrowski, Vienna, Va.; Pruitt Seafood, Washington, D.C.; Linda Robertson, JUD Tile, Vienna, Va.; Jon Rowley, Fishworks, Seattle, Wash.; Safeway Stores, Inc., Landover, Md.; Bert Saunders, WILTON Armetale, New York, N.Y.; James Simmons, Washington Fish Exchange, Inc., Alexandria, Va.; Greg Smith, Nikon Professional Services, Washington, D.C.; Straight from the Crate, Inc., Alexandria, Va.; Sutton Place Gourmet, Washington, D.C.; Triple M Seafood, Pompano Beach, Fla.; West Coast Fisheries Development Foundation, Portland, Ore.; Williams-Sonoma, Washington, D.C.; Tere Yow, Vietri, Inc., Chapel Hill, N.C.
The editors wish to thank the following for their donation of kitchen equipment: Le Creuset, distributed by Schiller & Asmus, Inc., Yemasse, S.C.; Cuisinarts, Inc., Greenwich, Conn.; KitchenAid, Inc., Troy, Ohio; Oster, Milwaukee, Wis.